<u>WHILE SEWING SANDALS</u>

TALES OF A TELUGU PARIAH TRIBE

MADIGAS SEWING SANDALS.

[*Frontispiece.*

WHILE SEWING SANDALS
TALES OF A TELUGU PARIAH TRIBE

EMMA RAUSCHENBUSCH-CLOUGH

Published by

Facsimile Publisher
12 Pragati Market
Ashok Vihar, Ph-2
Delhi-110052
facsimilepublisher.com

Distribution Network
gyanbooks.com
India, USA, Canada, UK, Australia, France

ISBN : 978-93-5324-521-4 (HB)
First Published, New York

2nd Impression 2020

Printed at: Gyan Press, Delhi.

While Sewing Sandals
Tales of a Telugu Pariah Tribe
Author: Emma Rauschenbusch-Clough

While Sewing Sandals

Tales of a Telugu Pariah Tribe . . .

BY

Emma Rauschenbusch-Clough, Ph.D.

Member of the Royal Asiatic Society of
Great Britain and Ireland

NEW YORK CHICAGO TORONTO

Fleming H. Revell Company

Publishers of Evangelical Literature

To

MY FATHER

Professor A. Rauschenbusch D.D

WHO HAS PASSED ON TO ME THE HERITAGE OF
ANCESTORS WHO SOUGHT AND SUFFERED
FOR TRUTH THIS STORY OF A TELUGU
PARIAH TRIBE IN SEARCH
FOR TRUTH IS AFFECTION-
ATELY INSCRIBED

Preface

MANY a day I passed with a group of Madigas before me, listening to their legends, hearing about their cults. I received glimpses of life in the Indian village community, and I felt the heart-beat of the religious life of the common people of India.

The Madigas are among the humblest and most despised of the Pariahs of Southern India. They are the leather workers in the Telugu country. For centuries they have tanned hides, sewed sandals, prepared leather buckets for the wells of the Sudras, and made trappings for their bullocks. And all their search for truth was carried on *while sewing sandals* with their hands.

I have described what I heard from them. In some respects I found myself on untrodden ground. With regard to the Matangi cult, the Chermanishta sect, the cult called Perantalu, and the several Reform sects which came to my notice, I cannot quote the researches of others in corroboration of that which I found among the people.

The story of the mass-movement toward Christianity has, I trust, retained in its English rendering some of the quaintness, the distinct originality, that was so fascinating to me, when I heard it from my Madiga friends. Many of them I had known for seventeen years. Memory carried me sufficiently far back to make their reminiscences seem very real and lifelike.

It was my intention not to draw on the fund of information gathered in hearing my husband, Rev. J. E. Clough, D.D., tell of the early days at Ongole. I wanted to put myself into the place of the Madigas, and to see the situation with their eyes. My husband's side of the story, therefore, still remains to be told.

I am grateful to him and to several friends in India, who furnished me with opportunity to meet Madigas living at a distance, whose memories were stored with tales of the Telugu Pariah tribe, to which they belonged. A Eurasian gentleman in Ongole helped me in gathering legends direct from the people. In my search in libraries in India and in London I have been most courteously aided, and from several members of the Royal Asiatic Society I have received valuable suggestions. All this I would gratefully acknowledge.

E. R. C.

LONDON, 1899.

CONTENTS

PAGE

A HISTORY NOT WRITTEN IN BOOKS

1 An Ancient Tribe 1
2 Traditions of a Tribal Head 13
3 The King of the Matangas 21
4 Scattered and in Servitude 31
5 Transformed into a Buffalo 45

ANCIENT MOTHER-WORSHIP

1 The Curse of Arundhati 53
2 The Initiation of a Matangi 62
3 The Matangi in Legends and Stories . . 77
4 The Fiend Mahalakshmi 90
5 Secret Meetings and Midnight Orgies . 103

CHRISTIANITY AND THE GURUS

1 A Search for Truth 113
2 Six Gurus in Succession 130
3 The Silence of Ramaswami 141

PAGE

FROM NASRIAH TO CHRIST

1 Nasriah the Reformer 157
2 Longing to See God 167
3 His Mother's Curse 183

BATTLE-GROUND FOR TWO RELIGIONS

1 Through much Tribulation 201
2 Not Peace, but a Sword 218
3 The Persecutor and His End 247

THE POWER OF CHRISTIANITY

1 A Great Calamity 271
2 A Modern Pentecost 285
3 Conclusion 302

REFERENCES 311

INDEX 315

LIST OF ILLUSTRATIONS

	PAGE
Madigas Sewing Sandals	*Frontispiece*
Buffaloes Bathing in a Tank	49
The Matangi, her Attendant, and the Bainundu .	70
Mahalakshmi and her Attendants	91
A Hindu Guru	144
Idol Worship	164
Madigas with their Drums	215
Poleramah and her Brother	250
Famine-stricken Christians	274

A HISTORY NOT WRITTEN IN BOOKS

AN ANCIENT TRIBE
TRADITIONS OF A TRIBAL HEAD
THE KING OF THE MATANGAS
SCATTERED AND IN SERVITUDE
TRANSFORMED INTO A BUFFALO

AN ANCIENT TRIBE

When it came to pass, twenty years ago, in the town of Ongole, in Southern India, that ten thousand Madigas turned to Christianity in one year, there was questioning as to the causes of this movement. Devout minds saw in the baptism of two thousand two hundred and twenty-two in one day a modern Pentecost, and were filled with wonder and gratitude.

Others enquired with interest concerning accompanying circumstances and conditions, and when they heard of the famine which immediately preceded this movement toward Christianity, they were satisfied that they had here the moving cause. The desire to enter upon the experience of the Christian was considered to stand in direct proportion to the hunger that was gnawing. But the mass movement toward Christianity continued long after the famine was over. Sixty thousand Madigas are to-day counted as Christians. The Madiga community of a part of the Telugu country has become Christianized.

During the months which I spent in listening to tales of this Telugu Pariah tribe, both from Christians and non-Christians, I ever kept in mind the questions that might be asked by those who looked upon this Pentecostal event in modern missions from different standpoints. I looked for traces of a direct manifestation of God's Spirit upon the minds of men, and I found them. At the same time I was on the alert to detect the special features of environment that made a mass movement toward Christianity possible. I found these also.

The methods of historical criticism are singularly inadequate when they approach the phenomenon of God's Spirit working in the hearts and minds of a multitude of men. Reason, with its limited range of comprehension, cannot analyze, differentiate and explain that which belongs to the realm of faith. God's power is there. He whose faith delights in the sublime mysteries of God is satisfied to know that God's presence is manifest. But he also who sets aside the supernatural, because beyond the reach of analysis and criticism, and looks upon this movement among the Madigas from the sociological standpoint, will find that after he has reckoned with each factor of environment, an unknown factor still remains, and this factor is the divine power inherent in the Gospel of Jesus Christ.

Much seemed to me explained when I found that the nucleus of the Ongole Mission was formed by men who, long years before the missionary came to Ongole, had become dissatisfied with the cults of the Madiga village, and had carried on a search for truth by listening to the teaching of Hindu Gurus. They took the first step out of polytheism into theism by learning from their Yogi teachers that there is one God and that He is spirit. This represented spiritual gain of a high order. But what was more valuable than this, perhaps, was the receptive attitude, the thirst which could not be quenched. When the Gospel of Jesus Christ came to these men, there was a gratitude in their hearts that formed a tremendous impetus toward Christian activity.

Another condition which I found had largely affected the movement toward Christianity among the Madigas was their strong family cohesion. During the course of many centuries, through famines, pestilence and warfare that swept over the land, the Madigas have retained their distinctness as a tribe. We see them to-day, despised as Pariahs, yet forming a unit among the many other units which comprise the social life of India. They preserve their traditions; they have a cult which is distinctively a Madiga cult; they even have their own village jurisdiction on a tribal basis.

In going back to the earliest days of the Ongole Mission, I found several centres from which the influence radiated, and they were family centres. The man who first brought the tale of the strange new religion had to be identified as belonging to such and such Madiga family; he was invited to the evening meal, and the family listened to him as a family in the hours of the night. There was family deliberation as to whether this religion was true and right, and the family stood together to meet the petty persecutions that followed so surely in many a case.

There were men also who met Jesus Christ in the way, alone, and went home to face the hard ordeal that falls to him who is cast off by his family as a heretic, as a promulgator of a strange new religion. These men were determined that their families must come with them. They went to distant relations; they journeyed to reason with the connections of the wife. The sense of family cohesion was so strong upon them, the thought that they might lead a separate life henceforth seemed unnatural and scarcely to be entertained.

Family cohesion was the channel through which spiritual truth spread rapidly. It was also the channel that carried precepts directed toward uplifting of a social nature. When the Sudras saw how Christianity proved in the case of the Madigas a power to make life on earth more wholesome and clean, they considered it social redemption of a tribal nature. They said: "This religion has come to them. It would be well for us also if a religion came to us that would educate our children and make us respected." Christianity found in tribal characteristics a powerful ally.

The Madigas are without doubt a very ancient

tribe. It is possible that they are among the aboriginal tribes of Southern India who are descendants of the Kolarian race, a very rude and primitive race, which may have occupied India previous to the advent of the Dravidians. It is also possible that there were several migrations of Dravidian tribes. Perhaps the Madigas were among the earliest of the Dravidian invaders, but yet of the same stock. In support of this hypothesis I would point to the fact that the legends and cults of the Madigas bear the family resemblance of Dravidian tribes, and that in their hamlets the same self-government exists, on a small scale, which marked the ancient Dravidian village community. I have not found proof of equal weight to support the theory that they are of pre-Dravidian racial affinity.

If scholars were agreed concerning the racial origin of the Dravidians, we might proceed to assign to the Madigas their place in the human family. But we meet with conflicting theories. Both Blumenbach and Haeckel, the one by the characteristics of the skull, the other by the structure of the hair, find that the Dravidians are neither Caucasian nor Mongolian, but have their place between the two races. According to Haeckel's hypothesis, the Dravidians advanced into India from the south, from that continent Lemuria, which he considers man's primeval home, now sunk below the surface of the Indian Ocean. Dr. Logan finds an Indo-African element in the Dravidian physiognomy, and supposes that a negro race overspread India before the arrival of the Scythians. Dr. Caldwell applies the philological test. He claims that the Dravidians came from the north, because vestiges of Dravidian dialects mark the pathway. A Scythian invasion preceded the Aryan invasion. The Dravidian dialects bear distinct affinity to the Scythian group of languages. He argues, therefore, that the Dravidians are of Scythian race. The racial origin of the Dravidians is not yet ultimately settled.

Concerning the Indo-Aryans, scholars are agreed that they are of Caucasian race, pure and simple. They are the Sanscrit-speaking branch of the Indo-Germanic races, and entered India from the north, perhaps about the year 3000 B.C. Wars and conquests marked their course in Northern India.

The ancient Rishis in the hymns of the Rig Veda praise the Vedic god of battle: "Thou, O Indra, hast with thy weapon smitten the mouthless Dasyus; in the battle thou hast pierced the imperfect-speaking people."

When, at a later period, their southward progress began, they had neither weapons in their hands nor appeals to Indra on their lips. They employed the arts of peace. Aryan hermits settled in the southern forests, and became the friends and instructors of the Dravidians. Previous to this contact between Aryans and Dravidians we have no means of knowing anything about the ancient Dravidians.

They were evidently not to be despised by the proud Aryans, for they had considerable resources. Governed by kings, they lived in fortified cities, fought with weapons, and possessed much wealth. Four cognate languages were spoken by the Dravidians, the Tamil, Telugu, Canarese and Malayalim. It is doubtful whether they had a literature anterior to Aryan influences. In abstract ideas they were deficient, but for every other range of ideas their languages afforded ample means of expression. They were a practical people. The Aryan colonists were compelled to acquire the Dravidian dialects and to content themselves by introducing Sanscrit terms into the local vernaculars.

In their social organization the two races differed widely. Among the Aryans of the north the caste system was already developed when their colonists began to migrate to the south. The only distinction known to the Dravidians was that of high and low, patricians and plebeians, as is found in all primitive communities. The Aryans had their strong Brahminical hierarchy, while the priests of the Dravidians were self-created, respected according to their skill in magic and sorcery. The Aryans burned their dead; their widows were not allowed to re-marry; they abhorred the eating of flesh and the spilling of blood. The Dravidians, on the other hand, buried their dead; their widows re-married; they ate flesh of all kinds, and no ceremony could take place without the excessive use of strong drink and the spilling of blood.

When the two races first came in contact there seems to have been antagonism in religious lines.

The Brahminical settlers complained in the exaggerated language of the East concerning "the faithless creatures that inject frightful sounds into the ears of the faithful and austere eremites." Hiding in the thickets adjoining the hermitages, "these frightful beings delighted in terrifying the devotees." At the time of sacrifice they came and snatched away the jars, the flowers and the fuel, they cast away the sacrificial ladles and vessels, and polluted with blood the cooked oblations and offerings.

The mingling of tribes and races and the fusion of cults and religious systems which constitute modern Hinduism was then in its infancy. The Madigas were there and bore their part. With their Matangi cult they reach far back into antiquity. Leather-workers by occupation, they are among the lowest of the Pariah tribes. Yet the social and religious customs found among them to-day have their root in the India of thousands of years ago. The first contact between Christianity and this ancient tribe must, therefore, be of a unique character.

TRADITIONS OF A TRIBAL HEAD

The Madigas proudly point to Adijambuvu as their great ancestor. He was the "grandfather of the Madigas," who was created "six months before the world began." This places Adijambuvu as to time, for in India "the world began" when the Aryans made their conquests, and this man, who was "the first Madiga," was one of those who were in possession of the soil when the invaders came.

Now Adijambuvu was very great. No matter what Rama wanted to do about war, he first went and asked him, as patriarchal head, for his advice, and then did what he said. Though of high estate when the Aryans first came in contact with the sons of the soil, the day of humiliation came to Adijambuvu. He fell from his height.

There was in those days a cow, called Kamadhenu, for she was the "cow of plenty." A boy, whose name was Vellamanu, tended the cow, and she gave much milk. Adisakti, the primeval energy worshipped by the aborigines, permitted the gods to drink the milk of Kamadhenu.

The boy, Vellamanu, desired exceedingly to taste of the milk. But the gods said: "You shall not by any means partake of it." He would not rest satisfied. One day he lay down as if sick. By stealth he took the pot from which the gods had drunk the milk, poured water into it and drank it. He said to himself: "If the milk tastes so good, how must the meat taste?" Kamadhenu became aware of his evil intentions. At the very thought that any one should desire to eat her flesh, her spirit departed, and she fell dead.

The gods heard what had happened. They came to the spot and found Kamadhenu dead. What should be done? They went to Adijambuvu and said: "You are the greatest among us. You must divide her into four parts." He did so. One part he retained for himself, one part was given to Brahma, one to Vishnu, and one to Siva. They took their parts and went away.

Ere long the gods came back and said, "We must have the cow again." They brought their three parts, and called for Adijambuvu's part. But the boy, Vellamanu, had meantime cut off a piece and was boiling it. As it bubbled in the pot a particle of the meat rose with the bubbles and fell into the fire. He took it up, blew against it, so that the moisture in his breath touched the meat, and put it back into the pot.

Adijambuvu took his part of the cow, and with the other three parts proceeded to create a new cow. But, alas! the flesh that had been boiled and breathed upon could not be replaced. Kamadhenu was not as before. Loose skin was hanging down from her chin, the flesh that had formerly filled it was gone. She was reduced in every way. From her proud stature of two heads, four horns, eight feet and two tails she dwindled down to the present size of the cow.

The gods said, "Adijambuvu has to come down from his height and be beneath us." Thus the day of his humiliation began. He dug himself a well, and the boy, Vellamanu, dug another, for caste difference rose between them.

Such is the legend of the "grandfather of the Madigas." But who was the boy, Vellamanu, whose interference had so great an effect? There is among the Pariahs a priestly caste called the Valluvas, who preserve to this day, with great faithfulness, a species of learning that is akin to the priestly lore of Brahmin sages. Vestiges of Sanscrit learning are found among them, which point back to a time when the Aryan hermits were on friendly terms with the aboriginal tribes, willing to teach them. It seems when the days of separation and caste feeling came, the Valluvas formed the link between the old and the new.

The boy, Vellamanu, had milk to offer to the gods. Adisakti regarded the gods with favour and allowed them to drink, for the Aryans partook of the cults of the aborigines; they imbibed aboriginal ideas. But when the boy, Vellamanu, would share the drink of the gods, he showed himself unworthy. The lust of meat filled his mind. It was the old bitter contention between Aryan and Dravidian, because the latter eat flesh, that wrought the change in the early friendly relations. The cause of the change was social incompatibility.

I searched in books for a trace of Adijambuvu, and found several references where he is taken out of the region of the legendary, and transplanted through his descendants into our own times. There is among the Madigas of the Canarese country a priestly tribe, called Jambu, who never intermarry with the laity, and live entirely on their contributions. A high priest, whose office is hereditary, takes frequent rounds through the country, collecting money and admonishing his followers. It is not difficult to frame the supposition that the tribal head in time became the priestly head. As the tribe scattered, the priestly hierarchy was not sufficiently powerful to make itself felt among the portions of the tribe that had migrated to some distance. Two subdivisions of the Madigas mentioned in the census, the Jambava and Jambavanta, may be direct descendants of Adijambuvu.

The legend said the "grandfather of the Madigas" was the respected adviser of Rama in matters of war. I turned to the *Ramayana*, the great Sanscrit epic, to find a trace of him there. The poet speaks of "Jambavan, chief of the bears," who is probably Adijambuvu, the first Madiga. Decked out in poetical garb, to harmonize with the other heroic figures, Jambavan is honourably mentioned, and his opinions are recorded at length.

The poet of the *Ramayana* sought a picturesque effect by naming the hosts, who helped Rama in war, by their totems. Possibly the hosts of monkeys and bears worshipped these animals. But since Dravidian dynasties had animals as their devices, the Gheras an elephant, the Pallavas a tiger, it seems probable that the tribe of Jambavan had the bear as a device and was named by the poet accordingly. The forest Dandaka extended probably from Bundelkhand south to the Krishna River. The army of Rama was thus gathered in the region where the Madigas to-day are scattered.

Rama, the hero of the *Ramayana*, was a prince of the house of Oudh. He was sent into exile, and after dismissing his charioteer on the confines of civilization, he entered the great forest Dandaka. Sita, the faithful wife of Rama, a beautiful type of the Aryan woman, accompanied him, and bore contentedly the hardships of life in the jungle for love of her husband. But Ravana, King of the

Rakshasas, who dwelt on the island of Lanka, Ceylon of to-day, came and carried her away. Rama, distracted with grief, called upon the chieftains of the powerful tribes of the country to aid him in the rescue of Sita. Sugriva of the monkey host was his most powerful ally. But there were others also, conspicuous among them Jambavan, chief of the bears.

A great army of combined forces is soon on its way, bent on the rescue of Sita. As they travel south, they reach the sea, and behold! On the other side is Lanka, where the wicked Ravana has imprisoned Sita, the beautiful wife of Rama. The powerful hosts of monkeys stand on the shore of the sea, and as they realize that they must bound over the deep, they waver.

They are addressed by Sugriva, the great general of the army: "Ye hosts of monkeys, unfold your respective powers in bounding!" There are rejoinders from several, but no one offers to perform so great a feat of valour.

Finally Jambavan speaks forth: "Formerly my prowess in leaping was great. But I have waxed old, and my vigour sits feebly upon me." He cannot undertake the leap, but when the commander proposes to go before all, "the exceedingly wise Jambavan" tells him that the dignity of the master bids him order his servants to go, but not to stoop to obey an order which he himself had given. His advice prevails, and ultimately "the highly heroic monkey Hanuman" is convinced that it is due to his courage and reputation that he should be the first to undertake the leap.

With a display of much strategy and valour, Sita is rescued from the palace of the powerful Ravana, who, with his host of Rakshasas, is laid low.

All other legends concerning the Madigas contain the element of degradation, of subordination. "Jambavan, chief of the bears," and Adijambuvu too, in his original state, stand high. No one looks down upon them. In their primitive greatness they hold their own. Alas for the heavy lines that were drawn to mark their descendants as outcasts!

THE KING OF THE MATANGAS

If the Madigas were once a tribe, with their tribal chief at the head, renowned in legendary and poetical stories, it would seem probable that somewhere in authentic historical records there should be some mention of them. But not a trace of them is to be found anywhere that could be called historically beyond a doubt.

This, however, is not surprising. The Dravidians had no literature previous to the time when Aryan hermits settled among them and reduced their languages to writing. Had the learned sages taken an interest in writing chronicles, and putting on record their experiences in dealing with the tribes among whom they had settled, ancient Indian history would not to-day offer so large a field to conjectures and suppositions. The learning of the Aryans was expended on religious and metaphysical writings, on their law-books and the two great Sanscrit epics. Much of historical information may be gleaned from these sources, but it must be accepted with some reserve, for religious motive and poetical license are not conducive to an impartial statement of events.

Yet the ancient inhabitants of India were not without the very human desire to be remembered by their descendants. They sought a way which seemed to them the most permanent to hand down to posterity a record of their deeds. On stone tablets and copper plates, on monumental stones, the pedestals of idols, and on the walls and pillars of temples they engraved their names their victories, and the defeat of their enemies. The student gleans from this source a history of dynasties and other bare facts of history which are, to a degree, trustworthy.

If a record of the Madigas, as a tribe among other tribes, could be found in an inscription, it would at once take their history out of the region of the merely conjectural and legendary and place it on a somewhat firm foundation. I thought I had found a record of this kind. It dates back to the year 634 A.D., when Mangalisa, a king of the Chalukya dynasty, conquered the Katach-churis, one of the early Dravidian dynasties.

The inscription is engraved on a stone tablet let into the outside of the wall of a temple at Aihole in the Canarese country, and contains the following sentence: "*His younger brother Mangalisa, whose horses were picketed on the shores of the oceans of the east and the west, and who covered all the points of the compass with a canopy through the dust of his armies, became king. Having with hundreds of scintillating torches, which were swords, dispelled the darkness, which was the race of the Matangas, in the bridal pavilion of the field of battle, he obtained as his wife the lovely woman who was the goddess of the fortunes of the Katachchuris.*"

As to whether there is a reference to the ancestors of the Madigas in the above sentence depends on the interpretation of the word *Matanga.* The word has several meanings. It may signify a "tribe of the lowest caste." Scholars agree that the term *Madiga* is derived from the ancient term *Matanga.* Moreover, there is a large sub-division of the Madigas called

Matangi. And the Madigas of the Canarese country call themselves *Matangi-Makkalu*, which means "children of Matangi."

But the word may also signify "an elephant." Eighteen years ago Mr. Fleet, who found the inscription and deciphered it, interpreted it as "some aboriginal family of but little real power." In a revision of his work, a few years ago, he says, "Examining the verse again, I consider that the components of it are connected in such a way that the word *Matanga* must be taken to denote 'the elephants of the Katachchuris.'" Thus the supposition that the Madigas were meant in the inscription is rendered very doubtful.

There is nothing left to do but to turn to traditions, to prize the legends that afford some clue to the understanding of social and political developments. In India, where memory is trained to an unusual degree of retentiveness, and fathers pass on to their sons what they, in turn, had heard from their fathers, legendary accounts are trusted to a greater degree than elsewhere. Professional singers, too, go about among the people and entertain them with poetical accounts of the happenings of bygone days. And thus the past reaches over into the present, and is kept from being utterly forgotten.

Some highly poetical accounts are to be found in Sanscrit stories concerning a king of the Matangas. They give a glimpse of the attitude of the Aryans toward the aborigines. And though the descriptions are in the exaggerated language of the East, they give the leading characteristics of an uncultured, aboriginal tribe.

Thus a Sanscrit author, Banabhatta, who lived about the year 606 A.D., describes in the story of *Kadambari*, the leader of the Cabaras, Matanga by name, as follows: "He was yet in early youth; from his great hardness he seemed made of iron; he had thick locks curled at the ends and hanging on his shoulders; his brow was broad; his nose was stern and aquiline; he had the heat warded off by a swarm of bees, like a peacock-feather parasol."

As the young leader, Matanga, approaches with his followers, who, as the poet says, numbered many thousands, they seemed "like a grove of darkness disturbed by sunbeams; like the followers of death roaming; like the demon world that had burst open hell and risen up; like a crowd of evil deeds come together; like a caravan of curses of the many hermits dwelling in the Dandaka Forest." Such, to the Brahmin poet, was the terrible aspect of the wild throng.

And then in his exhaustive description he characterizes them much as a proud Brahmin to-day, with a shrug of the shoulder, might give his opinion concerning the outcaste Madiga: "Their meat, mead, and so forth, is a meal loathed by the good; their exercise is the chase; their Shastra is the cry of the jackal; their bosom friends are dogs." A wild, aboriginal tribe these followers of Matanga were! Beyond this the poet discloses nothing.

Again we come upon a king of the Matangas in a volume of Sanscrit tales. They were compiled by Somadeva Bhatta, who lived about the year 1125 A.D. He states that he used an older and larger collection of tales in writing his *Ocean of the Streams of Story*, thus placing the date of the action of the tales centuries previous to his compilation.

He tells the marvellous tale of Durgapisacha, "the demon of the stronghold," whose aid is sought by a noble king and his ministers in accomplishing a certain quest. This chief of the Matangas is of terrible valour. Kings cannot conquer him. He commands a hundred thousand bowmen of that tribe, every one of whom is followed by five hundred warriors. When King Migrankadatta looked upon the country of the Matangas, he said to his ministers: "See! these men live a wild forest-life like animals, and yet, strange to say, they recognise Durgapisacha as their king. There is no race in the world without a king; I do believe the gods introduced this magical name among men in their alarm, fearing that otherwise the strong would devour the weak, as great fishes eat the little."

Now when the King of the Matangas heard the wish of King Migrankadatta, he assured him that it was a small matter to accomplish, and politely adds, "Our lives were originally created for your sake." The stranger was a man of high caste, yet he sought to please the chiefs who were willing to serve him. "He even went so far as to make the King of the Matangas eat in his presence, though at a little distance from him." Thus, though powerful, and in a position to render valuable aid, there was a very definite line of division between the noble Aryan Rajah and the head of this aboriginal tribe.

As the tales proceed we are told of a Chandala maiden, "who surpassed with the loveliness of her face the moon, its enemy." A noble prince beholds her as she charms into submissiveness an elephant, that was roaming at large and killing many men. He goes home to his palace, "his bosom empty, his heart having been stolen from it by her." His parents inquire for the maiden, and learn that she is the daughter of Matanga, King of the Chandalas. The queen, his mother, asks, "How comes it that our son, though born in a royal family, has fallen in love with a girl of the lowest caste?" She is told that the maiden is probably of a higher caste, and for some reason has fallen among the Matangas. Several stories follow to support this theory.

A messenger is sent to the King of the Matangas, who approves, but demands that eighteen thousand Brahmins must first eat in his house. The god Siva had pronounced a curse on him that his lot should be cast among the Matangas until eighteen thousand Brahmins had been fed in his house, when he should again be restored to his former position in a higher caste. The Brahmins were persuaded in a dream to go and eat. They expressed their willingness to do so, but demanded that the food be cooked outside the quarter of the Chandalas, for then only could they eat. The curse of Siva was removed, and the prince married the maiden, now of high degree.

Weighed down by Brahminical inventions and exaggerations as these stories are, they are not without touches that seem true to life. King Migrankadatta, as he reflects on the desire of men, though they live like the animals of the forest, to recognise some one as king, does not seem to distinguish between the Aryan conception of a king and the tribal chieftainship of the aborigines. King Durgapisacha had not the power of the Aryan Rajah to levy taxes, to decide matters of life and death, and to live in isolated splendour. As chief of the tribe of the Matangas he probably had the best and largest holding of land, with servants and a suitable retinue. He lead his tribe in warfare. On matters of administration he consulted the heads of families.

King Durgapisacha, rendered somewhat stilted and unnatural by Brahminical interpretation, yet bears resemblance to Adijambuvu, the grandfather of the Madigas.

SCATTERED AND IN SERVITUDE

Various causes may have worked together to scatter the tribe of the Matangas and to give to their descendants a home on the outskirts of the villages throughout the Telugu country. There were probably inter-tribal wars in ancient times. Subjugated by some stronger tribe, the Madigas may have been forced into servitude by the rights of warfare. On the other hand, the search for occupation may have been the motive that led to emigration, until the old tribal home was forgotten.

Only in faint outlines can a picture of ancient India be drawn, as it was before the Indo-Aryan appeared, who introduced gradually but surely a new order of society. Vestiges of the customs of the ancient Dravidian village community still remain. They form a clue to the primitive state of society in which caste-distinction was unknown, where all worked together to meet the needs of the community, and none were despised as outcasts.

The territory of Southern India was probably divided among Dravidian clans, or tribes, who had their chiefs and their tribal constitution. The members of the clans settled in groups, forming villages, that they might aid each other, for tigers and other wild animals of the jungles were plentiful, and there were clannish wars that called for united resistance. Each village sought to maintain its interests and provide for its simple wants. There was division of labour, and, in turn, each family received an allotment of land, or was paid in kind, so that all had enough.

The hereditary head-man, a distinctively original feature of the Dravidian village system, and the prototype of the Munsiff of to-day, was given the best and largest holding of land in the village. For the worship of the deity there was a similar provision. The village craftsmen and menials were not paid by the job; they were given a small holding of land rent free, or they received a given number of sheaves of corn or measures of grain. In the simple village community the leather worker was probably a respected artisan. He had his rights and they were respected; for the arrangements of the community were made on the principle of mutual service.

But the time came when great Dravidian kingdoms arose in the extreme southern part of the peninsula. Conquests were made. There were petty Rajahs at first, until all were subjugated by a powerful dynasty. The villages now became tributary to some central government, which levied taxes and demanded tribute. New features were introduced into the Dravidian village. The head-man, with his old tribal authority and small magisterial power, was overshadowed by a kind of second head-man, the Karnam of to-day, who was necessarily literate, and could keep accounts and make out statistical returns. The days of simple wants met in simple ways were over.

Gradually the influence of the Aryan colonists began to make itself felt. The primitive Dravidians were filled with respect when they saw the intellectual superiority of the Brahminical hermits who settled in their forests. They became pupils, and looked up to them as masters. With a natural curiosity and interest they must have listened to the stories told by the strangers in their midst concerning the northern country whence they had come. They heard of the feats of valour performed by the warlike Kshatriyas, the rulers of the north. Vaisya traders came among them, representing the third caste of the twice-born Aryan.

There was a fourth caste in the north, the Sudra caste, composed of the Aryan servants and some of the more civilized aboriginal races who had been conquered by the invaders. The free, unconquered Dravidians of the south stood far above the Sudras of the north. Yet, by some process, not unsupported probably by the talent of the Brahmins for flattery and intrigue, the Dravidians did not regard in the light of dishonour the place accorded to them as Sudras in the scale of caste-distinction.

For the Madigas there was no place within

the pale of the Indian caste-system. In the primitive Dravidian village it was probably a matter of amicable settlement that the leather workers should live together in a group of houses on the outskirts of the village. Not until the harsh lines of the Aryan caste-system were drawn was the group of dwellings transformed into the hovels of the outcast. And the rulers of the land demanded service of the Madigas under provisions closely resembling slavery.

The condition of the Madiga community has probably changed more during the past thirty years under British rule than during many centuries previous to the influence of Western civilization. Old men have told me of conditions which had undoubtedly been in force since time immemorial, of which their sons knew nothing by experience. A glimpse of the life of the Madiga in the Indian village community, thirty years ago, furnishes, therefore, a link to the past all the more valuable because the ancient lines are fast disappearing.

In the old days, when there were petty Rajahs, tributary to some powerful dynasty, it happened occasionally that the Rajah or his minister, the Dewan, came to visit his domain. It was convenient for them, at such times, to find everything provided for them in the places where they halted. The potter was expected to provide pots; the washermen's service was required; the Munsiff brought eggs and milk; and the whole village drew on its resources. In turn for this service, the Rajah made grants of land to each according to the value of the service required of him on such occasions. To the Madigas fell the lot of being the burden-bearers; for, when roads were few and often impassable, the camp-baggage was placed upon the Yettis, to be borne from place to place. They, too, received a grant of land, seldom, it seems, more than four acres; and it yielded but little, for the Madigas had not the bullocks to plough, nor the time to watch their growing crops.

Moreover, Yetti-service was not confined to the time when the Rajah came, or when he sent his Dewan; those in authority could at any time demand the service of the Yettis, and it was always service without pay. When the Karnam came to a village to collect the tax for the Rajah, the Yettis had to stand at the entrances of the village and see that neither man nor cattle went out. After the tax had been gathered, the money was tied into the scant clothing of the Yetti, and, two together, they went long distances to deliver it at the centres of the districts. They looked poor and ragged, and none suspected that they had money concealed about them. Arrived at the place of destination, they dared not approach the Brahmin accountants within. They stood afar off, and held the package high in their hands, till a Sudra servant came out to deliver it to the Brahmins within, who would have considered it pollution to accept anything from the hands of a Madiga direct.

There were daily recurring tasks for the Yettis. They had to gather wood for fuel for the Karnam's household. If there were letters to carry from village to village, the Yettis were pressed into service. If any one wanted a guide to point the way on an untravelled road, the Yettis were placed at his disposal. Travellers who wanted burden-bearers made their request to the Karnam. He furnished the Yettis, but kept the payment for himself, giving them, at their clamorous entreaties, a mere fraction of what they had earned. If ever they dared to refuse to work, they were ill-treated, their few heads of cattle were driven to the pound, and the misery of their condition was only increased by their remonstrance.

Some of the petty Rajahs ordered their Karnams, or Dewans, to look for able-bodied Madiga men on the fields or in their huts, and to secure them for menial service. Accordingly they took men away from their homes, and, if they resisted, they were treated cruelly. This mode of procedure was resorted to especially when a Rajah desired to dig a tank in order to irrigate a district of land. A Madiga told me that his father was taken away from home by the servants of a Rajah, and forced to work on the tank at Podili for months. They threatened that they would beat him or bind him, if he demurred. He received only enough to provide himself with food while digging. To his family there was nothing to send; they had to shift for themselves as best they could.

The taxes levied by the Rajahs were an additional heavy burden. After the grain had been harvested and cleaned, and the Sudras had measured out to the Madigas the part of the harvest that was theirs, on the principle of mutual service, the servants of the Rajah came and put a seal upon it. The women could not use it for cooking until after they had paid their tax. If they bought a cloth, about one-eighth of the cost had to be paid as tax, and often the Rajah's servants went to the washermen to look over the clothes, and if any were found without the seal, they took them away.

The relation of the Madigas to the Brahmins was, and is, serfdom, without the relieving feature of a paternal interest. The Sudras, on the other hand, though they have every opportunity for oppression, take the part of friends and protectors. The Madiga family that does not bear to some Sudra land-holder the relation of serf to master is considered unfortunate, and finds it difficult to get food sufficient to ward off starvation. The Madiga serves the same Sudra family from generation to generation. When there is a marriage in the Sudra family, the Madiga celebrates the event by a marriage in his own hamlet. The Madiga does not go upon a journey, nor does he enter upon any serious undertaking, without consulting his Sudra master. He is at the Sudra's bidding day and night. At seedtime and harvest he is at hand, and while the crop is growing he watches in the field to chase away the crows in the day and to guard against thieves in the night. In turn for his labours he is paid, not in coin, but in kind. The measures of grain are meted out to him according to the plentiful or scant nature of the harvest.

The leather-work for the Sudras is also done on the principle of mutual service. When among herds of cows and goats, kept by the Sudra landholder, a head of cattle dies, the Madigas are called. They secure the hide, and, in turn, they tan the leather, sew the sandals for the Sudra, make the trappings for his bullocks, and do any other leather-work that is required. In parts of the country where the soil is dry and hard, the

Sudras dig deep wells in their fields and with the help of bullocks draw the water to the surface, where, through little channels, it irrigates the whole field. For this purpose large leather buckets are required, and the Madiga community finds frequent employment in making them and keeping them in repair.

By right of trade the Madiga secures not only the hide of cattle, the carcase too is his. As death is always caused by disease, never by slaughter the flesh is poisonous and loathsome in the extreme, especially in a country where decomposition is a rapid process. In this phase of their occupation lies the beginning and the end of the Madiga's degradation. Hungry many a day in the year, living by the month on one meal a day, seldom in possession of the means to buy meat fit to eat, they do not shrink from the loathsomeness of the meal which is furnished them by the carcase that is theirs by right of trade. It is this to which their legends point as the curse with which their tribe has been laid low. Perhaps in the early days, when Jambuvu, "the grandfather of the Madigas," lived, it was less difficult to obtain food to quench hunger. A famine, such as is told of in ancient records, that swept the land and almost depopulated it, may have taught the Madigas to eat the flesh that poisoned the blood in their veins, that rendered them filthy and an object of abhorrence to the Hindu, who is forbidden to kill and eat flesh of any kind. And afterwards he was unable to raise himself from abject poverty.

The Madigas are miserably poor. I enquired into their condition in several districts, and found that, striking an average, only one-third of the Madiga population is above absolute want. But the possessions of this favoured one-third, too, are readily enumerated. Each family lives in a hut built of stone laid in mud, and covered with thatch, giving a room about ten feet square. By way of furniture there are a few cots, made of a frame of wood with twine woven across, and a few low stools. Earthen pots, large and small, used as cooking utensils, a few baskets, a few brass utensils, a stone to pound the rice, and a roller to grind the curry-powder complete the arrangements of the household. There may be a cow, perhaps a buffalo, several calves and some fowls. Each member of the family has two suits of clothes' and a cotton sheet for covering at night. The women have strings of beads and a little cheap jewellery. Perhaps a bamboo box hangs from the beam that supports the roof of the house, containing red clothes to wear when invited to festivals. A family whose possessions are as above specified is considered a thrifty, well-to-do Madiga family.

But two-thirds of the Madiga community have only a portion of the above-mentioned possessions. Cattle is lacking, there are no cots, no brass vessels, no red clothes for holiday attire. A few suits of clothes constitute the outfit of the whole family. If any of them need to make themselves presentable, they wear the better part of the wardrobe of the family. Many a day in the year they go hungry, glad if they can get a meal of boiled grain of a kind that is cheaper even than rice, and a little pepper-water poured over it to give it a relish.

Crushed by serfdom, debased by poverty, the Madigas yet uphold among them village jurisdiction on a small scale. The Sudra village has its headman, the Madiga hamlet has its Madiga chief.

He represents the Madiga village on special occasions. If hospitality is to be extended, it is his roof that must shelter the guest. Disputes and quarrels are brought to him for settlement. If public opinion in the Madiga hamlet is roused against the misdeeds of one who has his home in it, the Madiga headman, perhaps with several of the older men to assist him, passes judgment, levies a fine, or expels the evil-doer from the borders of the village. The fines pass into the hands of the Madiga headman, as remuneration for the expense borne in extending hospitality and the time given to his administrative duties.

Thus, though scattered and in servitude, the Madigas cling to their ancient tribal organization. They submit to the Munsiff and the Karnam; they bend low and even cringe before those who have authority over them. But, in their own hamlet, they give to one of their number the dignity of representing the interests of all. They thus prove their affinity to the stronger Dravidian tribes. And the tenacity of their tribal character becomes the vehicle of civilizing and educating forces at the present time.

TRANSFORMED INTO A BUFFALO

The Komati Chetty sits in the bazaar behind his wares. He has baskets of grain before him. There is a basket of tamarind, another of red pepper. Not everything is displayed and temptingly laid out for the eyes of questioning purchasers on his verandah. There is a door behind him, which, when open, reveals bags and baskets filled with wares stored away.

Perhaps he deals in cloth, in needles and thread and scissors, in beads and glittering ornaments made of paste diamonds and rubies. Ask him for a few yards of tape, and he dives into the well-stocked "go-down" that opens from his verandah, pulls out a package, opens it before you and displays tapes of different widths. He brings out fine muslin and flowered chintz, and says, "Buy, missus, verry cheap." He even has a china pug dog to show you, and cheap playthings that are marked "Made in Germany." Ask him the "proper price," and he mentions three times the amount which he can justly claim. Bargain with him, decide finally that you do not want his wares, and he will hand them to you at a reasonable cost.

The Komati is often a wealthy man. He has money, and lends it at high interest. The women go to him and buy the rice for the evening meal, and the various spices that go to make a good curry. Pariah women, too, must come to buy. Sometimes the scant cooley which the family has earned is not enough to supply food for all, though they buy the cheapest kind of grain. Then they go into debt with the Komati, and he keeps them in fear and anxiety until the debt is paid.

It would not occur to any one that there could be a connection between the wealthy, prosperous Komati and the poor, despised Madiga if peculiar customs did not exist that point to some kind of tie between them. The Komatis are not pleased with a reference to these customs. The ill-will of other castes, they say, spreads these tales about them.

The marriage ceremonies of the Komatis are

generally as elaborate as their wealth will permit. Friends and relatives are invited to sumptuous feasts. But, though the Madiga would not be a guest in any way desirable, he must be invited, lest ill-fortune befall the young couple. And the Madiga is far from coveting such an invitation; he considers it unlucky and insulting. Should a Komati dare to extend it openly, his messenger might be treated roughly at the hands of the irate Madigas.

The Komati waits for a time when it is not likely that the Madigas will see him. He takes the iron vessel with which he measures the grain and makes his way to the Madiga hamlet. Hiding behind one of the houses, he whispers into the vessel, "In the house of the small ones (Komatis) a marriage is to take place; the members of the big house (Madigas) are to come."

But this is not sufficient. The light with which the fire is kindled during the marriage ceremony must come from the house of the Madiga. There is obstinate refusal when asked. Perhaps the men of the Madiga hamlet grow angry when they hear of the request. Strategy must be employed, the light which the Madiga refuses to give must be taken from him by stealth, to satisfy custom.

There must be some reason for these customs. Major Mackenzie observed them even as far south as the Mysore district, where the Madigas have emigrated. He suggests that the connection between two such different castes as the Madigas and Komatis may lie in the fact that both worship the same goddess. The Komatis have as their caste-goddess the virgin Karnika-Amma, who destroyed herself rather than marry a prince, because he was of another caste. She is represented by a vessel full of water, and during the marriage ceremony is brought in state from her temple and is placed on the seat of honour in the house. The Madigas claim Karnika as their goddess, under the name Matangi, and object to seeing the Komatis take her away.

This is certainly significant, showing that there is connection between the two castes, not only by social customs, but also by similar religious interests. I have heard a legend which may throw some light on the subject. It was told

BUFFALOES BATHING IN A TANK.

[Page 49.

by a Komati, and, like most Indian legends, includes the element of the impossible.

There was once a Brahmin who, contrary to the rules of caste, lived with a Madiga woman. He was versed in the arts of the magician, and, by his magic, he transformed her by day into the body of a buffalo; at night she was again a woman. They had eleven children.

One day the Brahmin was called away on urgent work. He called his children and charged them to care for the buffalo, to untie it and take it to the field to graze.

The children did not know of the transformation which took place every day. Thoughtlessly they drove the buffalo before them to pasture, and when it would not go as they wished they beat it with a stick. But the buffalo was old and weak. It fell down and died.

The father came home, and the children told him that the buffalo was dead. He asked how it died, and said: "Alas, the buffalo was your mother! As an expiation of your crime, go and cut up the buffalo and eat it." The Komatis are said to be the descendants of these children.

Once a year the Komatis shape a lump of dough, made of rice-flour, into a four-legged animal, to represent a buffalo. Each member of the family takes a little of it and eats it. This ceremony is called Nabsanimudda.

The legend and this household ceremony have something in common. It is not impossible that the Komatis may be of mixed descent. I looked for information concerning them in the *Manual of Administration of the Madras Presidency*, and found that they are said to have emigrated from some place in the north, a few authorities mention Penoocondah, which was a place of importance under the Vijayanagar dynasty. There is evidently some doubt as to the locality from which they have sprung, and nothing definite is known of their origin. They claim to be purer Vaisyas than other subdivisions of the trading-castes, and are divided into many clans.

Neither Komatis nor Madigas are pleased with the connection between them. Strange, therefore, that it is so enduring.

ANCIENT MOTHER-WORSHIP

The Curse of Arundhati

The Initiation of a Matangi

The Matangi in Legends and Stories

The Fiend Mahalakshmi

Secret Meetings and Midnight Orgies

THE CURSE OF ARUNDHATI

There was once upon a time a Brahmin who had done many evil deeds. He believed that he could receive the expiation of all his sins if he found a woman who had faith sufficient to transform sand into rice. He inquired among all castes, but nowhere was there a woman who had this supernatural power.

Finally he came to the Madigas. Now the maiden Arunzodi heard of his quest. She appeared before him and said: "I can do it, but I am of low birth. My father is wont to kill cows and eat them. We are outcasts."

The Brahmin was exceedingly glad, and he besought the maiden to grant his request, notwithstanding her low degree. He argued with her, but Arunzodi said, "When my elder brother comes home and sees you, his wrath will be great, for we eat meat."

This did not convince the Brahmin; he insisted, and finally Arunzodi yielded. He brought sand and she put it into the pot. He broke iron into small pieces, and this also she put into a pot. She saw what she had in the two pots, but so great was her faith, she proceeded to boil it.

With great anxiety the Brahmin stood by and watched. When Arunzodi had finished cooking, behold! one of the pots contained boiled rice, the other was full of curry. Certain that he had found his saviour, the Brahmin asked for Arunzodi in marriage.

But now the elder brother came home. He was enraged when he heard what had happened, and threatened to do violence to the Brahmin and to Arunzodi, his sister, also. No one among the Madigas befriended them, for all said: "She is bringing a stranger into our households and our caste! Turn them out! Away with them!"

Then it was that Arunzodi, before the eyes of all, rose to heaven. And she cursed them, saying: "You shall be the slaves of all. Though you work and toil, it shall not raise your condition. Unclothed and untaught you shall be, ignorant and despised from henceforth!" Thus Arunzodi cursed her people as she rose up, and they and the Brahmin were left standing and gazing after her.

The Madigas cannot forget Arunzodi. The Dasulu often tell the story of her faith, and of the curse with which she cursed her people, which, alas! has been fulfilled. And as the Dasulu recite they accompany themselves with instruments.

There are other legends about Arundhati, which is the Sanscrit form of the Telugu word *Arunzodi* and means "everlasting light." One is that Arundhati was re-born as a Madiga woman, and married the sage Vasishta, the brother of the great Agastya. She bore him one hundred sons, ninety-six of whom reverted to the Pariah state, because they disobeyed their father, while the other four remained Brahmins. Among the hymns of the Rig Veda there is a bridal hymn. At the close this verse occurs: "*As Anusuya is to Atri, as Arundhati to Vasishta, as Sati to*

Kausika, so be thou to thy husband." It is significant that in Sanscrit dictionaries both Arundhati and Matangi are mentioned as the "wife of Vasishta," making the two identical.

When they have a wedding, the Madigas specially remember Arunzodi. After one of the Madiga Dasulu has performed the marriage rites, as ancient custom demands, it is thought well for the prosperity of bride and bridegroom if they, accompanied by their friends, go out under the starlit heaven to greet Arunzodi. Though she may not be visible, her cot is always there, and all can find it. The four bright stars in Ursa Major are the feet of her cot, made of very precious material. The three stars on one side of the four are thieves, who are stealing three feet of the cot, and have already pulled the cot crooked, for the four feet form an irregular square. And so the young couple look at the cot, and say, "Arunzodi cannot be far away!" They bow and worship, for they believe that she has power to bless.

Arunzodi is not the only Pariah woman who, in legendary history, is vested with the power of working miracles by reason of great faith. Very different is the story of the meek Vasugi; yet she too took sand and boiled it, and it became rice.

Vasugi was the wife of the Tamil sage and poet Tiruvalluvar, who, according to tradition, was a Pariah weaver, living near Madras about 1000 or 1200 A.D. There was, in his day, a famous Sanscrit Academy in Madura, to which all Tamil scholars of that day belonged. When the Pariah bard presented himself, with his thirteen hundred couplets, his want of caste was made an excuse for his exclusion. Yet down to the present day his chief work, the Kurral, is considered by Hindus of all classes a work of high moral and religious worth.

To the poet Tiruvalluvar the maiden Vasugi was offered in marriage by her father. He was inclined to accept her, for he considered domestic virtue the highest virtue, but resolved first to try the maiden's gifts. "If she will take this sand," he said, "and boil it into rice for me, she shall be my wife." Vasugi took the basket of sand from his hands. She felt sure that what the holy man ordained was possible and right. Her faith was great. She boiled the sand, and as a virtuous woman has power with the gods, a miracle was wrought, and she brought the sage the rice for which he asked. She became his faithful, obedient wife.

The years passed, and the poet's fame spread. Attracted thereby, a stranger came to his cottage and asked the question so much discussed at that time in India : " Which is greater, domestic life or a life of asceticism ? " The sage courteously entertained the stranger, but gave no reply to his question. He left him to judge for himself the nature of his domestic life. It happened, one day, that the poet called his wife while she was drawing water from the well. She instantly came, leaving the bucket hanging midway in the well. Again, when she brought him his morning meal of cold rice, he complained that it burnt his mouth. Without question or hesitation she began to fan it. And when, in broad daylight, he dropped his shuttle, while weaving, and called for a light to seek it, she lit the lamp and brought it to him.

The stranger exclaimed : " Where such a wife is

found, domestic life is best. Where such a wife is not, the life of the ascetic is to be preferred!" When the meek Vasugi, the poet's wife, closed her eyes in death, it was said of her that she had never during her whole married life questioned her lord's command. The character of Vasugi, meek, gentle, humble, is in accordance with the spirit of the Kurral, the Pariah poet's chief work.

To what extent the tradition of Vasugi was influenced by Aryan ideals of the perfect woman is a question. The discussion concerning the value of asceticism speaks of Aryan rather than Dravidian influence. The story of Vasugi, like that of Arunzodi, is not free from Brahminical impositions. There are few legends in India that do not bear the imprint of Brahminical extravagance, and the ill-concealed effort of the twice-born to magnify their own supremacy. A legend, therefore, which by its simplicity and artlessness proves its purely Dravidian origin is the more to be prized. The following legend was taken from the oral tradition of the Coorgs, one of the smaller Dravidian tribes.

In ancient times there lived in the Malabar

country six brothers and a sister. They went together to Coorg, but the brothers were not pleased because the sister came with them, and they decided to spoil her caste. On the way they were hungry, and said to the sister, "Prepare us some food." She replied, "There is neither fire nor rice." They said, "We will give you rice, but you must boil it without fire." She replied, "I will boil it without fire, but you must eat it without salt." To this the brothers agreed.

The sister saw a cow and milked her, letting the milk fall into the vessel of rice. Then she went to the bank of a river, buried the pot in the sand, and it began to boil. The brothers awoke from their sleep and ate.

Later, while sitting together, chewing betel, they said, "Let us see whose betel is the reddest." They all spat out the betel into their hands, looked at it, and the brothers threw it behind their heads. The sister, deluded by this, threw the betel back into her mouth and went on chewing. The brothers now said she had lost her caste. She was excessively grieved and wept bitterly.

One of the brothers threw an arrow, and ordered

his sister to go with it and stay where it fell. She assumed the form of a crane and alighted on a Pariah, working in the rice fields. He became possessed with a devil and ran towards the mango tree, where the arrow was sticking. A temple was built around this tree, where the Coorgs still worship the sister of the six brothers, especially at her annual feast.

The Coorgs, like the Tamils and Telugus, are ot Dravidian stock. There is a family resemblance in these three legends. In each the chief figure is that of a woman, who, in the ordinary labour of cooking rice, is endowed with miraculous gifts. These legends of three Pariah women stand in a line with the cults that are Mother-worship. The Dravidians believe that women may come in touch with mysterious forces, and that if they have sufficient faith they can compel these forces to be subservient to them.

THE INITIATION OF A MATANGI

As I stepped out upon the verandah one morning, I was greeted by the salaam of my old friend, Konikaluri Yelliah. The dazzling whiteness of his turban emphasized the dark hue of the face beneath, which beamed in expectation of the things that were to come.

"Did you come walking all these sixty miles?"

"How could I walk? Am I not an old man? By your leave I came by bullock-bandy."

"And what have you to tell me now?"

"Whatever you give leave, that will I tell."

This was the polite reply which I had heard many a time. It had happened repeatedly that my questions, far from bringing to light valuable material, only revealed the fact that there was nothing to draw forth. I regarded Yelliah, as he sat facing me, as an experiment.

"Tell me," I said, "about the old days."

"My mother, Ammah, was a Matangi."

"And what is that?" I asked.

"A Matangi is a Madiga woman, who is possessed by Ellama."

"And who is Ellama?"

"She is Adimata, the mother who was from the beginning."

By this time I had straitened myself. I dipped my pen into the ink with an air of business. I took my note-book, and I said, "Now, Yelliah, begin at the very beginning."

And Yelliah began far back with his great-grandmother, who was a Matangi. His grandmother was not invested with the power. He was his mother's eldest child, and when he was about three years old something strange happened to her. She was well, and had been going to her work as usual, when, one Adivaramu, being the first day of the week, after the offering of food had been placed in the Ellama idol-house, she began to act in a peculiar way.

She sat apart at meal-time, and refused to eat. It was harvest-time, and for two weeks she went to the fields as usual, but aside from the grain, which she ate as she worked, she would not partake of food. The Sudras, for whom the family worked, noticed this. The whole village began to watch her closely, for she looked this way and that, and laughed to herself. They said, "What does it all mean?"

It soon became a matter of discussion in the community, for there were many who worshipped Ellama. No matter whether any one was a Sivite or a Vishnuite, he yet thought it well to worship Ellama. When it was decided, therefore, that a council should be called to investigate whether this woman was really invested with the power of Ellama, a very general interest was shown. Sudras and Brahmins came, but the man who was head of the council was the headman of the Madiga village, who, as such, had the function of entering the Ellama idol-house once a week with offerings of milk, butter, and fruit.

The test agreed upon was that the Bainurdu, who is the minstrel in the Ellama sect, should recite the story of Ellama in the presence of the woman. If Ellama's power had come upon her, she would dance, inspired by the goddess; if it was an evil spirit that possessed her, the story would not affect her. Without loss of time the test was made; and as soon as the minstrel began the young woman danced, and not only she, but her husband and other members of the family also danced, and thus it was evident that Ellama's power possessed the family.

All were now convinced that they had a new Matangi in this woman. It was considered an event, for Matangis were rare, only one or two in a Taluk. It was decided that an old Matangi from an adjoining Taluk should be called to initiate the new Matangi into the rites of the office. The family had to bear the expense of the initiation, about sixteen rupees, which necessitated a debt; but they did not hesitate, for they knew that afterwards there would be great gain. An atmosphere of expectancy and anticipation was abroad in the community.

There lived a Reddi in the place, who was chief of the Reddis, one of the branches of the Sudra caste. Years before he had had a serpent made, life-size, of silver, gold, copper, and various metals, and then he, and a number of villagers as witnesses, had gone to Sulvesanama Kona, where the Gundlacumma River flows through a cave, and where there is a famous place of worship. Here the Reddi fulfilled certain conditions, and went through initiatory rites, for which he received a certificate from the officiating priests. His wife had gone with him, and had also met all conditions, so that she, too, could take a prominent part in the worship of the snake, when, after their return home, they were asked here and there with the serpent.

The great day came when the old Matangi arrived. The Madiga headman went into the little thatch-roof house, sacred to Ellama, and took out the pot, hung to the roof, that contained coins and shells and other articles emblematical of Ellama and her sons. The pot was taken to the village-tank in the morning, and left in the water all day, a man remaining near by as guard. In the evening all went to take it out of the water, worship it, and take it back to the village. One goat was killed near the water, another half-way to the house, and a third after reaching the house, where the blood was painted over the door-frame. The Reddi had brought his serpent and placed it, with its hood spread, where the offerings of rice could be piled up around it.

That same night, after the serpent had been worshipped, the old Matangi and the Reddi's wife sat down together on the back of a goat. It lay down with the weight, but was dragged three times around the spot where the serpent and all the offerings were. Instruments were played, and the bystanders danced the wild dance of possession. Whatever trouble or sickness there was among the people would, it was believed, fall upon the goat and die with it. It was half dead, after being dragged three times around the circle, and was then taken to one side and killed.

On the next day all the rice and other offerings that had been heaped around the serpent were cooked by Sudras; for Brahmins too were coming to eat, and if Sudras cooked it, the caste prejudices of all were respected. There was a feast, and then all returned to their own houses. The old Matangi also went home. The new Matangi had been passive throughout, had simply looked on. She and her family worshipped Ellama for one week, and then went to their work as usual. She showed no further signs of possession. Only when stories of Ellama[1] were recited, she and others of the family began the dance.

During the year that followed the family and others of the Madigas worked and saved, and laid up grain, and contracted debts to meet the initiatory rites that were to follow. They could not accept help from the Sudras, or any one else, for the Matangi must come from the Madigas. It is a Madiga affair, and while other castes may share, they cannot have any initiative. A new pot was made for Ellama; shells and pebbles were brought from the sea; water from the Krishna River was brought to wash them.

Before the initiation could take place, however, a final test was ordained, to prove that the woman was really worthy of the office. On the floor of a house a figure in three parts was drawn, with white, red, and yellow powder. In one part the serpent had its place, in the second the Ellama-pot, and in the third the new Matangi was seated. A little earthenware pot was placed in each corner, painted with saffron and red dots, representing Ellama, and filled with buttermilk. Threads were then tied to the pots, brought to the roof and back again, crosswise, four times.

After these preparations had been completed, the Bainurdu began to recite Ellama stories, accompanying himself with his instrument. The possession came upon the woman, but she could not rise up and dance, she had to remain seated and contain it within herself. If she could not do this, she was not worthy. The strings tied across furnished the proof, for if she moved they would break, and the buttermilk in the pots would be spilled. In due time the Bainurdu said soothing words, and the possession slowly disappeared.

A crowd of people had stood by as witnesses, and great was the feeling of relief when the new Matangi had stood the test and proved that she would be able to carry her office with dignity. Again the old Matangi was called; this time to stand by and instruct her colleague in office.

First she was decked like the old Matangi, with new clothes, her face and arms were painted with saffron, rice was tied around her waist, and a wreath of margosa leaves was hung around her neck. As her insignia of office, a basket was placed in her left hand, a stick in her right hand, and two small plates, one containing yellow saffron, the other red powder, were held by a woman who was her female attendant. She stood in the middle of the crowd, took buttermilk into her mouth, passed it on a bunch of margosa leaves, and sprinkled it on all who stood near. It was believed that whoever was thus sprinkled would be cleansed from all defilement and pollution; for even the touch of a Matangi is thought to have power. In the night the Reddi's wife and the new Matangi sat on the goat together; again the serpent was worshipped, and there was great feasting on the day following.

After this the new Matangi went about with her husband, performing the ceremonies of her office in the villages of the Taluk. Her husband was passive, for men can never assume the *rôle* of a Matangi.

THE MATANGI, HER ATTENDANT, AND THE BAINUNDU.

[*Page* 70.

The followers of this Matangi were displeased because she allowed herself to be photographed, yielding to persuasion and a substantial present.

Such was the story of the initiation of a Matangi as told to me. I enquired for legends concerning the Matangi cult, and found one which is not without additional information.

There lived, once upon a time, a king whose name was Dundagheri Rajah. His wife was Jamila Devi. When the king was holding court one day, a beautiful maiden appeared before him. She was an incarnation of the goddess Parvati, the consort of Siva. The king extended his right hand to catch the maiden, but she moved away from him. He and his people followed in pursuit of her, but she receded, and finally disappeared into an ant-hill. The king sent for diggers, and ordered them to dig till they found the girl, and offered large rewards. They began to dig, but soon found that the ant-hill was hard as stone. The king then sent for stone-cutters, and the queen offered them still greater rewards. They too failed. Then the king grew angry, took his spear, and drove it into the ant-hill. The spear pierced the skull of the maiden, and as the king pulled out the spear, the brains of the girl began to ooze out and blood began to flow. The king and all his followers, at sight of this, fell into a swoon.

The maiden then came out of the ant-hill in great majesty and of divine proportions. She held the heavens in her left hand (the basket to-day represents this), in her right hand she held Adisesha, the great serpent (the stick is now substituted for this). She held the sun and moon as plates, in one of which she caught the spilt blood, in the other the scattered brain. Upon the foreheads of the people, that lay in a swoon, she made a mark with the brain and another with the blood. Therefore the Matangi to-day has two plates, one with yellow saffron, the other with red turmeric, with which she marks the foreheads of people. After all those who lay in a swoon had been thus marked, they recovered, and saw the goddess before them in the form of a maiden. The king and queen took her into their house. She was afterwards married to the sage Jamadagni, and had five sons.

To say that the Matangi cult is a species of Sakti-worship would be correct, but it would not touch upon its real significance. Saktism is the worship of the female energy in nature, and is multitudinous in its forms, though nearly all have their root in Parvati, the consort of Siva. It cannot be said that it is of simply Aryan origin, to be traced back to the union of Dyaus and Prithivi, Heaven and Earth, in the hymns of the Rig Veda. Nor can it be said that the worship of the female principle in nature is exclusively of Scythian origin. It is a form of worship that constitutes an integral part of nature-worship, as it appears among many of the races of antiquity. The Matangi cult has its root far back in ancient mother-worship, in the age of the Matriarchate. Some of the religious rites of that age find expression in the Saktism of to-day.

I would point out that in the Matangi cult some of the most ancient modes of worship of the human race converge.

As far back as the records of the race can be traced, serpent worship is found as a means with which the human intellect sought to propitiate the unknown powers. Whether invariably the serpent is so prominent a feature in Matangi worship as in the case related to me I doubt; but the two cults were evidently thought to blend harmoniously. In the legend of the Matangi the maiden disappears into an ant-hill, generally the home of serpents, coiled up in the passages which the ants have burrowed for themselves, feeding on the inmates. Moreover, the stick in the hand of the Matangi represents Adisesha, the primeval serpent, showing that the two cults are linked together.

Tree worship in ancient times went side by side with serpent worship. Traces of this also are found in the Matangi cult. When the power of Ellama descends upon an unmarried Madiga girl, the ceremony of marrying her to a tree is sometimes performed, leaving her free thereafter to do as she pleases. The wreath of margosa leaves around the neck of the Matangi, and the bunch of margosa leaves in her hand, with which she sprinkles the bystanders, may also be vestiges of a cult that has the same root as the groves of Baal and the sacred trees of the Teutons.

The rite of sacrificing a goat, after having dragged it three times around the hooded serpent, crushed by the weight of two women, one the representative of the Matangi cult, the other of serpent worship, is very significant. The practice of the Matangi to paint the foreheads of her worshippers with saffron and red, explained as being the brain and the blood of the Matangi, is equally significant. It points to human sacrifice, which has been intimately associated with serpent worship. The two existed side by side in India from the earliest time. Though the higher culture of the Aryan was opposed to the sacrifice of men, and the mild doctrines of the Buddhist were equally antagonistic to it, yet the British Government, even in our own times, has had to take steps to prohibit by law the vestiges of ancient rites of this kind that still existed among aboriginal tribes.

The Matangi cult illustrates the exceedingly complicated nature of modern Hinduism. Only the great antiquity of the cult can explain the fact that several other distinct cults have found a place in it. The desire to work out a scheme of salvation was the motive power that produced this readiness to adopt and assimilate other cults.

Though the Matangi cult is non-Aryan in character, the Brahmin has yet an interest in it. He, too, stands by to be sprinkled by the margosa branch of the Matangi, and be cleansed from evil. And in all the striving there is the hope that thus, perhaps, the soul may be saved.

THE MATANGI IN LEGENDS AND STORIES

After gathering from the Madigas all they could tell me of the Matangi cult, I turned to books to find corroborative evidence of the antiquity of the cult, to get an explanation of its rites and customs. I found that two scholars, Professor Wilson and Sir Monier Williams, give the same enumeration of Saktis: "Kali, Tara, Shodasi, Buvaneswari Bhairavi, Chinna Mastaka, Dhunavati, Vagala, Matangi, *i.e.* 'a woman of the Bhangi Caste,' Kamalatnika." The name of Ellama is here omitted, and the Matangi is given a place among the ten great Saktis. This does not coincide with the information I obtained about the Matangi. Perhaps these ten Saktis belong to Northern India, rather than to Southern India.

There is another enumeration of Saktis in a book which treats of the gods of Southern India. It is as follows: "Mariama, Ellama, Ankalama,

Bhadrakali, Pidari, Chamundi, Durga, Puranai, Pudkalai." Ellama here has a place among the great Saktis. The Matangi cannot be given a place among them because she is only the Pariah woman who is at times possessed by the spirit of Ellama.

The author who thus gave me some slight corroborative evidence was the great Danish missionary, Ziegenbalg. He wrote his book on *The Gods of Malabar* in the year 1713, and sent it to Germany for publication. He was informed that the project of publishing his book could not be entertained, that he had been sent out "to uproot heathenism, and not to spread heathenish nonsense in Europe." The great missionary was a scholar. His book, not published until 1867, contains information for which the student seeks in vain elsewhere.

While I failed to find a description of the Matangi cult, I yet found traces of the name in several books, in a way that served as a landmark. There was a degree of satisfaction in its recurrence, for the surrounding group of circumstances bore the mark of similarity. Wherever the name *Matanga* or *Maṭangi*, whether with masculine or feminine ending, occurred, there was religious aspiration, and with it the Chandala element.

The earliest mention of the name Matangi is to be found in the *Mahabharata*. It is not possible to give an authentic date in connection with this Sanscrit epic. Portions of it are of great antiquity, and the tradition of the sage Matanga probably belongs to the older parts. He was one of the limited number of renowned sages of Indian antiquity who were of degraded origin.

Matanga considered himself the son of Brahmin parents. One day, however, he made the discovery of his spurious birth. He was travelling in a car drawn by asses. They walked slowly, and in his impatience he goaded the colt. "It is a Chandala who is in the car; his wicked disposition indicates his origin," said the she-ass to the colt.

Matanga heard this, and immediately besought the she-ass to tell him what she knew of his origin. He learned that his mother was a Brahmin, but that his father was a Chandala. Determined yet to earn Brahminhood, Matanga entered upon a course of austerities. Indra, to whom he appealed, refused his request, because so high a position cannot be obtained by one who is born a Chandala. One hundred years of austerities passed, but were of no avail. After Matanga had stood on his great toe for another one hundred years, Indra relented to the extent of giving him the power to change his shape at will, and move about like a bird. This legend indicates the strength of the Brahminical hierarchy to exclude all who were not of purely Brahminical birth.

Centuries pass, and again we meet with a sage, Matanga, mentioned in the *Ramayana*, the second Indian epic, which is also of great antiquity. When Rama, the hero of the epic, enters the great forest Dandaka, he is told that he will behold in the forest the abode of the great ascetic, Matanga, who was feared by all. "Even the elephants, though they were many, dared not cross the threshold of his asylum." Matanga, and the ascetics with him, had departed to heaven in celestial cars, leaving an "immortal mendicant woman, by name Savari," who had been commanded to await the coming of Rama, because she would then attain to the abode of the celestials.

Rama comes; he speaks to the female ascetic, who appears before him with matted locks, clothed in rags and the skin of an antelope: "O thou of sweet accents, hast thou succeeded in removing all hindrances to asceticism? Hast thou observed the commandments and attained to mental felicity?"

She approaches Rama with the words: "Favoured with thy presence, my asceticism hath attained to its consummation."

She shows him the spot known as Matanga's wood, and the various wild fruits growing on the banks of Pampa, which she had collected for him. He has come to take possession of them. Her work is done, and she announces her purpose of renouncing her body and approaching "those pure-souled ascetics" on whom she had formerly waited.

In an excess of joy Rama exclaims: "O gentle one, I have been worshipped by thee! Do thou depart at thy ease and pleasure." Thus dismissed by Rama, she surrendered herself unto fire, and repaired to that holy region where her preceptors dwelt.

A more tolerant spirit by far is shown in this story, as compared to the previous one. The ascetic, Matanga, belonged to the day when Aryan hermits adopted conciliatory measures in the colonization of Southern India. With his disciples he formed a colony, but they do not seem to have dwelt in proud isolation. They honoured a Pariah woman by leaving her in charge of the deserted hermitage until Rama should come. They taught her to desire the heaven of Brahmin ascetics.

Again there is a gap of centuries, and we find in the *Puranas*, which rank next to the *Ramayana* in antiquity, a legend which, though it may not directly refer to the Matangi, yet marks the change which time had wrought. The Brahmin Rishis had realized that the worship of the gods of the Aryans did not appeal to the mind of the aborigines, yet they desired to control the religious life of all. Thus it came to pass that Siva, one of the lesser gods of the Aryan pantheon, in the evolution of centuries, took upon himself the stern qualities which the Dravidians revered in their deities. His consort, Parvati, became the form in which Sakti worship found expression. She is worshipped to-day in a multiplicity of forms, not the least of which is that of the Matangi.

The legend, to be found in the *Valavisu Purana*, is as follows: An ineffable mystery was once revealed by Parvati, the wife of Siva, and her son, Kartikeya. By way of punishment, they were to be re-born in an infinite number of mortal forms. But Parvati entreated that the severity of the sentence might be mitigated to one transmigration. This was granted. At this time Triamballa, King of the Parawas, and Varuna Valli, his wife, were engaged in special acts of devotion in order to obtain issue. Parvati condescended to become their daughter and assume the name of Tiryser Madente. Her son became a fish of immense size, roaming about in the sea. Swimming south, he attacked the fishing vessels of the Parawas, and threatened to destroy their trade. The king made public declaration that whosoever would catch the fish should have his daughter as a wife. The god Siva assumed the character of a Parawa, caught the fish, and was re-united to his consort. This legend is an attempt to bring Siva and Parvati into very close contact with the aborigines. The Parawas rank first among the tribes of Tamil fishermen of to-day, and were once a strong people and had kings.

A more elaborate attempt, on the part of the Brahmins, to explain the presence of this aboriginal cult by the side of Aryan deities is found in the legend of Ellama. Vishnu, who is distinctly a god created of Aryan conceptions, here appears incarnate as the son of Ellama, in the form of Parasu-Rama. Saivism and Vaishnavism thus converge in the person of Ellama, for she was the personification of Siva's wife, and the mother of an incarnation of Vishnu.

Ellama was the daughter of a Brahmin. Her life from her childhood was so pure and holy that a great Rishi took her to be his wife. Parasu-Rama and three other sons were born to her. Her chastity was so great that by means of it she was enabled to roll the waters of the river Kaveri in huge balls to the place where her husband performed the sacrifice, that he might use it. One day she saw the shadow of something in the ball of water which she was rolling, and looked up. She saw the Gandharvas, the celestial musicians, flying through the air, and she admired their beauty greatly. Next day the water refused to be rolled. The Rishi asked, "Why can you not roll the water?" She replied: "Yesterday I saw a shadow in the water, and, looking up, saw the Gandharvas flying through the air. Beyond this I know of no sin." The Rishi replied: "Your chastity is lost. A chaste woman would not have looked up and admired the Gandharvas."

He called upon his sons to behead their mother, but they replied, "She is our mother; how can we cut off her head?" Parasu-Rama only was willing to do it, and the father sent him to find his mother. She had taken refuge with the Pariahs, who refused to deliver her to Parasu-Rama. He, however, killed all the Pariahs, and brought the head of his mother to the Rishi, who, greatly pleased, asked, "Son, what do you desire that I should do for you?" He said, "I desire that you give back to me my mother!" The Rishi granted his request, gave him the head of his mother, and he went in search of the body. Among the dead bodies of the Pariahs whom he had slain he could not find the body of his mother. He therefore placed the head upon the body of a Pariah woman, and brought her back to life. His father, when he saw her, said, "She is now a Pariah woman." Both mother and son were sent away from his presence. Parasu-Rama became a mighty king, and Ellama became a goddess.

According to Ziegenbalg, the pagodas erected to Ellama in the Malabar country contain eight figures beside her own. One of these is Matangi, the Pariah woman, on whose body the head of Ellama was grafted. Another is Jamadagni, her husband, who ordered that she should be put to death. It was Jamadagni whom the maiden married, after she rose out of the ant-hill as Matangi. This establishes a coincidence in two legends.

The legends concerning the Matangi have received their most elaborate touches in the legend of Ellama. The next mention of her I found in books of local history and biography, where she stands forth in bold outline, in striking contrast to the mythical form of legendary productions. She is now "a female warrior of her tribe," and takes part in the capture of Kampula in the Carnatic by Mohammed the Third in 1338. Many warriors from the Telugu country fought under the hero Kumara Rama, and she was among them.

The Matangi seems to have been treacherous, and to have gone over to the King of Delhi, who was highly incensed at the cowardice of his commanders, and put a large force of his soldiers under the command of the Matangi. Not only did she herself go over to the enemy, but she persuaded a company of Telugu soldiers to fight on the Mohammedan side. In the early part of the conflict that ensued, Kumara Rama was successful, and drove the enemy back. Not until then did he hear of the treachery in his camp, and speedily proceeded to the scene of danger, where he encountered the Matangi. He seized her nose-ring, shook it, and told her that he "disdained to take the life of a woman." His bravest soldiers, surprised and overpowered by numbers, fell fast around him, and he was left alone. After maintaining the conflict for a long time, and killing many of his assailants, he himself was at last slain, and the Matangi cut off his head and carried it to Delhi.

The Matangi here has the power of her office. As Matangi she wielded a powerful influence over the Telugu warriors, which led the King of Delhi to regard her as a desirable ally. Kumara Rama's hesitation to kill her, in the heat of battle, was probably due to respect for her office, rather than for her womanhood. She was the embodiment of a cult which all held sacred.

Looking back upon the recurrence of the name *Matangi* at intervals of centuries, far back into almost pre-historic times, we find one continuous thread of evidence that the Aryan invader, as he confronted an aboriginal cult of peculiar strength and tenacity, sought to find a place for it, to control it, and conquer it. The first step is indicated by the legend of the sage, Matanga, who was refused the boon of Brahminhood, showing the strength of the Brahminical hierarchy to exclude one who was of partly Chandala origin. Next we receive a glimpse of the more conciliatory measures adopted by Aryan hermits in the colonization of Southern India. Later we have Siva, the god evolved partly of Dravidian ideas, and his wife Parvati, taking upon themselves the form that would endear them to some of the lowest of the aboriginal tribes. Not satisfied with this, not only Saivism is brought in close contact with the Matangi cult, but Vaishnavism also finds a way to gain a hold upon it. It might seem as if the Brahminical hierarchy had now absorbed this strange cult. Far from it. The bloody ferocity of the "female warrior Matangi" differs from the loquacious curses with which the Brahmin sages content themselves.

The aboriginal tribes have clung to their cults with a peculiar tenacity. In view of the fact that the Brahmins have interested themselves in the Matangi cult, it is remarkable that none of their religious conceptions have penetrated into it. The legends concerning it they have succeeded in moulding according to their ideas. The cult itself they have not been able to reach. It is an aboriginal cult.

THE FIEND MAHALAKSHMI

Short of stature, bent with age and nearly blind, our old gardener in Ongole still came every day to sit under the large trees in the heat of the day, or to watch others do the work which he had done during many a year. His favourite grandson frequently led him about, holding him by the hand. At other times he found his way through the garden paths alone, leaning on his staff, seldom at a loss to know where he was, for every foot of ground was known to him, every tree and shrub had been cared for by him in the years that had passed.

His memory went back to the olden times, and mingled with that which had happened in his own day were the tales which he had heard his father recount. He was distinctively one of the oldest inhabitants of Ongole.

"Tell me about Ongole when you were a boy, gardener," I said one day.

MAHALAKSHMI AND HER ATTENDANTS.

[*Page* 91

This opened the flood-gates of his recollections, and the incident which seemed to him of greatest importance and interest was given first.

"Ammah, when I was a boy, the Rajah of Goomsur was taken through Ongole by the British."

"Why did they do that?"

"He was their prisoner. There were many soldiers who guarded him. And the men of his own household, who were with him, could do nothing. After five days they moved on to Madras."

This Rajah of Goomsur had Mahalakshmi as his goddess. He had dedicated all his fortunes to her, and sacrificed to her all that her priests demanded. Every day she had to have the blood of two buffaloes, and much other food besides. It was said that sometimes she refused to be satisfied with anything but human sacrifice.

After he had been taken prisoner, the Rajah could do nothing more for Mahalakshmi, and she waxed angry. One day she approached him, and said :—

"You offer me nothing. What am I to do?"

The Rajah replied:—

"The English Government did me this evil. Go to them, spoil everything they have, bring cholera and smallpox to their regiments." The goddess left him, thirsting for blood.

Great trouble and distress came upon Ongole three days after the Rajah had passed by. Never before had any one in Ongole known what cholera and smallpox were, but now they learned and trembled. The wrath of Mahalakshmi was very fierce. She slew all before her. Twelve died on the first day after she had begun her work. Many more died during the weeks that followed. No one could count them all. Not a village in the region round about was spared. So great was the thirst of Mahalakshmi for blood, that when a man fell sick he died on the spot. She let none escape.

Many were numb with terror. Others said: "If Mahalakshmi must have blood, give her the blood of beasts. Let it flow in streams! Perhaps she will spare us while she drinks it."

Hundreds of sheep, buffaloes without number, were sacrificed. Shrines were erected to Mahalakshmi. Hands reeking with blood were raised in supplication by those who saw one after another in their households succumb. Men and women in the frenzy of excitement danced the wild dance of possession, while instruments were played all day long, and priests were busy saying mantras.

Gradually it became evident that the thirst of Mahalakshmi was quenched. She grew mild as the years passed, and sometimes men who seemed doomed escaped her hands and returned to life.

"And do you doubt," the old gardener asked, "that these things surely took place? Look around in Ongole and in all the villages, and see the Mahalakshmi shrines. Not one of them was there before the Rajah of Goomsur passed through, when I was a boy."

I looked up the matter, and I found that there was a curious blending of fact and superstition in the story of the old gardener. It is a fact that a rebellion took place in the State of Goomsur, about three hundred miles north of Ongole, in the year 1835. The Rajah was taken prisoner, and was brought to Madras, probably through Ongole. It is also a fact that the first epidemic of cholera in the Madras Presidency, within the memory of that generation, had broken out a few years before; so that in the perspective of later years the two events easily became identical.

It is a coincidence to be noticed that the people of Goomsur, who are Khonds and are of Dravidian origin, have a goddess called Jugah Pennu, who "sows smallpox upon mankind as men sow seed upon the earth." When a village is threatened with this dread disease, it is deserted by all save a few persons who remain to offer the blood of buffaloes, hogs, and sheep to the destroying power. Human sacrifice was not unknown among the Khonds. The character of Jugah Pennu is very like that of Mahalakshmi, even down to the hint concerning human sacrifice. Perhaps some of those who travelled in the retinue of the Rajah brought the germs of the disease to Ongole. The terror of the weeks that followed gave to the Rajah's sojourn and the outbreak of disease the relation of cause and effect in the minds of the people; and Mahalakshmi thus became one of the most dreaded characters in the demon-worship of Ongole.

Numberless are the fiends worshipped in the Indian villages who are thirsting for blood, or who are busy night and day maliciously planning to injure and destroy. If any one falls sick, if the crops fail, if cattle die, or harm of any kind befalls the village, it is considered the work of some evil demon, whose vengeance and hatred must be kept in check by offerings.

A Brahmin once told me: "The god Vishnu stays in his holy place, but Poleramah, Ankalamah, and a host of other fiends and demons have their eyes ever directed to this earth, and go about seeking whom they may destroy." Though of Aryan stock, he leaned decidedly in the direction of Scythian demonolatry when he tried to explain to himself the phenomenon of positive evil. "The one supreme god," he said, "is too good to do harm to any one. But the demons stay close to the earth, and to do evil is their delight."

I have found in my enquiries among the Madigas that they continue to worship demons of a locality long after the reason that led to the worship is forgotten. I could only conclude that in generations past a man or woman had died under peculiar circumstances, that the spirit was thought to be restless and wandering about, and that, for some reason, a certain margosa tree had been fixed upon as its home. So, in accordance with ancient Dravidian rites, a stone was placed under the tree, painted with saffron, adorned with the usual red dots and then worshipped. Sometimes these local swamis are the spirits of good men and women, who are revered as kind and beneficent deities. But they too may turn into angry demons and refuse to defend men, if they are offended by a lack of devotion and by the paucity of offerings from the worshipper.

Once only my oft-repeated question as to the reason why some local swami was so faithfully worshipped brought me a satisfactory reply. I thus learned the origin of a beneficent village deity.

Not many generations past, for she is still remembered, there lived a Sudra woman, Chalkaṃah by name. Her father-in-law was a wealthy man. With considerable outlay of money he was digging one of those large square wells, so often seen in Southern India, which have the fountain in the centre, and the four sides terraced by stone steps, so that those who would fill their pots with water could easily descend. The diggers had gone to considerable depth, but there was no water. What should be done?

There was much talk and deliberation in the village, for a well with a plentiful supply of water is a matter of much importance in an Indian community. The general opinion was that some swami, some higher power, was withholding the water. An attempt must be made to propitiate the swami. It was decided that the owner of the well and his daughter-in-law, Chalkamah, should offer sacrifice. She was a young woman in the full strength of her prime. Her husband was still living, and she was, therefore, a woman who has power with the swamis.

They took pots, rice, saffron, incense and firewood, and descended to the bottom of the excavation. There they cooked the rice, set up three stones in the spot where the fountain should appear, painted them with saffron and made the usual red dots on the surface. They laid the rice before the stones as an offering, burned the incense, and then worshipped the three stones as if they represented the deity withholding the water.

The two worshippers came away. They had climbed half-way out of the well when Chalkamah turned back. She had forgotten the copper cup which she had used in cooking. Descending again, she stood at the bottom, and as she bent to pick up the cup, behold! the water rushed forth to meet her.

Her father-in-law, still standing half-way, called to her, "Come up quickly!" An inarticulate sound came back as an answer. Again he called, and again the same sound rose up amid the rush of water. He dropped everything in his hands and turned to the rescue of Chalkamah. He called to her again, as he began to descend. Now there was a distinct answer: "Don't call me again!" Thus Chalkamah expired.

Many stood at the top of the well, and saw and heard all. They said, "She could have fled and escaped if she had wished!"

But the water was rising. There was great abundance for the use of the village. It was said of Chalkamah, "She must have been a holy woman or the water would not have rushed forth to meet her!" As a beneficent matri, who was supplying the village with water, she was henceforth worshipped.

A matri like Chalkamah belongs to the village. Similar worship as a household institution I found among the Madigas under the name Perantalu, meaning "a good and fortunate woman." I was told that other castes, too, worship Perantalu. In fact, I saw the significant yellow and red markings on the door of a Sudra house.

When a woman in a Madiga family dies who has been what the Madigas consider a virtuous woman, one who was devoted to the swamis, and leaves behind her at death a husband, it is believed that she will go where she will have easy access to the gods and can intercede for the family. Widowhood among the Madigas does not mean the life of privation that makes the widowhood of caste-women so pitiful a state. Yet the Madigas think a woman leaves this world under fortunate auspices when her husband is left behind to mourn her death.

To facilitate communion with the departed one, a place on the inner wall of the house is painted yellow with saffron; red dots are made on the yellow surface, and a necklace with beads attached is fastened in the middle of it. This becomes the shrine of the family, before which they bow every day, and especially when they propose to go on a journey or enter upon any new undertaking.

It is possible that the Perantalu is a local superstition, for I have not found it mentioned in books. Yet it stands in a line with other forms of Saktism. The spirit of a highly-favoured female member of the family is credited with mysterious powers of an occult character, with a control of the secret forces of nature. It is the mother-worship of antiquity in a form that makes it a household institution.

But I would suggest that another element is present in the Perantalu as well as other species of mother-worship found among the Madigas. There is a persistent recurrence of the yellow saffron and red dots everywhere. In the worship of beneficent matris, when fiends and demons are to be propitiated, in the Matangi cult, everywhere the yellow and red markings are a necessary adjunct. Many a time I have seen a stone under a margosa tree, with the markings on the surface, and frequently a necklace of beads hung around it.

Is it not possible that this points to human sacrifice? Both Brahmanism and Buddhism were opposed to human sacrifice, yet with great pertinacity the spilling of human blood, in order to appease the gods, has endured among aboriginal tribes, even down to our own times. The British Government has had to deal with the vestiges of the cruel rites.

The Abbé Dubois, one of the keenest observers of Hindu customs, wrote at the close of last century: "Old men have told me that this horrible custom was still practised when they were young. I have visited several places where these scenes of carnage used to be enacted." He says there is not a province in India where the inhabitants do not point out to the travellers places where their Rajahs offered up to their idols unfortunate prisoners captured in war. This was one hundred years ago.

In the *Kali-Purana* the god Siva lays down the rules for blood-offerings. By a human sacrifice, he says, his consort is pleased a thousand years. By the sacrifice of three human beings one hundred thousand years. Kali and Durga, both belonging to the ten great Saktis, are always represented with the evidence of their thirst for blood conspicuous in some way. Perhaps a necklace of human skulls adorns the neck, or the tongue is stretched forth to indicate the thirst for blood. Alas! for the gloom of such worship.

Of the tribe of the Matangas the poet Banabhatta wrote about the year 606 A.D., "Their one religion is offering human flesh to Durga." Perhaps there was a time when the victims for sacrifice were allowed to escape, and in their stead a stone was painted with yellow saffron to resemble human flesh, and the red marks took the place of the blood that did not flow. It was hoped the thirsty gods would be appeased by this substitute, especially if the reeking blood of goats accompanied it.

SECRET MEETINGS AND MIDNIGHT ORGIES

Saktism does not assume its most revolting form in the Matangi cult, nor in the worship of matris and fiends and demons. The frenzy of possession, the mad excitement of the dance, the slaughter of beasts, and the shouts of the bystanders, may be sufficiently hideous; but they are not an outrage upon human nature.

In the Chermanishta sect there are meetings that need the cover of darkness. Vague reports only reach the outer world of that which is done in secret.

Once a year the members of the Chermanishta sect meet in the house of one of their number. They may belong to any other cult or religion and yet come to this secret meeting. Religious distinctions and caste distinctions are wiped out for the time being. Strange to say, Brahmin, Sudra and Madiga are, during that night, on a basis of equality. But the utmost secrecy is required of all. In the morning all resume their own caste, and no one dare divulge the knowledge of the presence of the others during the orgies of the night.

As midnight approaches, the Guru enters the house of meeting; the rest follow, one after another. After all are seated, the Guru goes around with a vessel containing sarai, and lets each one take a sip. In the other hand he has a piece of meat, and touches the tongue of each. He himself finally eats and drinks of both. Then nine kinds of meat, previously cooked, are passed around: fowl, pigeon, pig, goat, cow, donkey, cat, dog and buffalo. Each one puts a little of each on a plate made of dried leaves and eats it, while sarai flows plentifully.

While eating, all sing: "*We have now severed both caste and family connection. We have joined together both ruling caste and servants. We desire to be saved by the Guru. This is the time.*"

The piece of meat, which touches the tongue of each, seems intended to wipe out every social distinction between them. Later in the night a woman is brought in—generally, it seems, a Madiga woman—and there are orgies that form a loathsome representation of the creative force in nature. At last the Guru announces the place for the next meeting, and all steal away silently, one after another, as they came.

The fact that the Madigas are admitted to the rites which join *kulapathi* and *dasulathi*, "ruling caste and servants," is not without its own significance. Perhaps the Brahmins learned the mysteries of the cult from the aborigines. The members of the sect claim that the deeds of the night are free from lust and vice, because the mind is filled with thoughts of worship. It is nature-worship in the most revolting form, and may well be called the most corrupt aspect of modern Hinduism.

Nowhere in books could I find a reference to the Chermanishta sect. I concluded that perhaps it was Sakti worship under a local name—perhaps the name of the Guru who first taught its rites in parts of the Telugu country. I thought it would have to be classified as a worship of Siva, because Saktism generally centres in Parvati, the consort of Siva. But I was told repeatedly, by those who claimed that they knew, that it was part of the Ramanuja sect.

An explanation was given me which is a mixture of fact and hearsay. My informants knew that there was once a great teacher, Ramanuja, who made disciples of all castes and of both sexes. He did not initiate his followers into the mysteries of his doctrines, but wrote them in a book, which he concealed from them. At the time of his death no one was with him, and the book of secret doctrines fell into the hands of the Brahmins, who characteristically kept it to themselves. But his other followers, too, wanted to know of the teaching of their Guru. Two of his disciples, who were women of the caste of dancing-women, and were, therefore, versed in the art of reading and writing, sought to meet the emergency by writing each a book. They claimed that these books contained the teaching of Ramanuja, imparted to them on his death-bed. From one of these books sprang the Ramanuja sect, from the other the Chermanishta sect.

This is a curious instance of the way in which the common people explain to themselves that which is beyond their comprehension. It is probably true that at the death of Ramanujacarya, who lived in the twelfth century, and was the first of a line of Vaishnavite reformers, the Brahmins took possession of his books. The abstruse reasoning which they contained concerning a triad of principles—the Supreme Being, the Soul, and Non-Soul—was not of a nature to satisfy the wants of the multitude.

His followers corrupted his teaching. The sect was divided into the northern and the southern school. The struggle between the two schools was fierce, and was really the controversy between Arminian and Calvinistic doctrine in Indian guise. The northern school claimed that the soul lays hold of the Supreme Being as the young monkey clings to its mother, of its own free-will. The southern school have "the cat-hold theory." They argue that the soul remains passive and helpless until acted upon by the Supreme Being, as the kitten remains passive until the mother-cat transports it from place to place.

Not only on the question of free-will did the Ramanuja sect divide, but also on the question of the place to be assigned to the consort of Vishnu. The northern school regard her as infinite and uncreated, like her consort, while the southern school maintain that she is simply a mediator, not an equal channel of salvation. The story told me of the books written by the two dancing-women probably points to this division of the Ramanuja sect.

There is incongruity in giving to a sect that inculcates a hideous form of Saktism a place among the followers of Ramanuja. The teachings of Ramanuja were moral. He forbade the use of animal food and intoxicating drinks. He probably came in contact with Christian missionaries, for his insistence on the spiritual equality of all men points to Christian principle. He demanded personal devotion to a personal god, and this god was Vishnu.

The secret orgies of the Chermanishta sect date back thousands of years previous to the time of Ramanuja. To find for them a place in the Ramanuja sect is simply an attempt, unconsciously put forth, perhaps, of finding in the more modern religious movements a place for an ancient cult.

CHRISTIANITY AND THE GURUS

A Search for Truth
Six Gurus in Succession
The Silence of Ramaswami

A SEARCH FOR TRUTH

I knew Bangarapu Thatiah seventeen years ago, when he was yet in his prime, honoured and loved by all. I saw him again when old age rested heavily upon him and his memory failed him when he tried to recall the happenings of yesterday. But when I asked him about the far-away past, his almost sightless eyes seemed to peer into the distance, and he told me many things.

"I called our Dora and he came," he said to me, and then relapsed into silence. I looked about on the mission-houses, the school-houses, and the busy activity of the mission compound. And I remembered how this man, many years ago, came to this spot, his heart burning within him, to see whether the white teacher had not come. He found it overgrown with cactus, and Gundla Pentiah living in a hut in one corner of the compound, a faithful man, who told him that the

Ongole Missionary was yet in Nellore, but was soon coming.

Thatiah's plea was the last link in the chain of circumstances that brought the Ongole Missionary to this place. He could justly say before the younger generation, when he leaned heavily on the sturdy shoulders of the young men, "I called our Dora, and he came."

I said, "Thatiah, tell me about the old days." He looked about helplessly, and one of the younger men said, "Grandfather, the Dorasani wants to know about the time when the Dora first came here."

"When the Dora first told me to go and preach, I said, 'How can I go about alone all the time?' But he said, 'Take your wife with you and you will be two.' After that Satyamah and I always went together. Sometimes she carried the bundle, sometimes I put it on my shoulder. What I preached, she preached; what I ate, she ate. Satyamah was always with me."

"Did not men persecute you in the old days?"

Thatiah's face, grown passive with age, brightened with animation, as he assured me, "No one ever abused me, no one persecuted me; men always treated me kindly and respectfully."

"They tell me that you were much with Rajayogi Gurus. Did you learn anything from them?"

"Did I learn anything from them? They told me that there is one God, and that He is Spirit; that He has created all things, and pervades all things. It was well that they told me this, and I believed it. But nothing satisfied my soul till I heard of Jesus Christ."

Thatiah told me this, without hesitation, as one of the facts of his life. He was too old for meditation. Thus I had the summary of Thatiah's search for truth. He had found a nugget of gold in the Rajayogi sect, but the pearl of great price he had found when he heard of the Christ.

Thatiah had, years before, written a sketch of his life, at the request of the Missionary. This was supplemented by the story of many a man, who could not tell of the old days without bringing in Thatiah at decisive points. A singularly pure and holy life this man led before the eyes of thousands of his people.

He was born when his parents were advanced

in years. The duty of caring for them fell upon him. It never occurred to him that he might learn to read. There was no one in those days who would teach a Madiga boy to read. He learned of his father to tan leather, and sew the sandals which the Sudras ordered.

In the time of his grandfather, a Guru of the Ramanuja sect had been invited by the family to come with the idols of Vishnu and perform sacred rites before them. This was repeated on special occasions, and the fees demanded by the priest were paid out of the scant earnings. When his father died, Thatiah took pride in having the funeral ceremonies performed according to the dictates of a Guru of the Ramanuja sect. This was considered an advance, both religiously and socially, upon the cults and customs of the ordinary Madiga.

Neither Thatiah nor any other Madiga has ever told me that he had gained in spiritual truth by joining the Ramanuja sect. The Madigas know nothing of the doctrines of the sect, nor do they see any deeper meaning in the several incarnations of Vishnu. This utter lack of apprehension concerning the tenets of a sect which they had joined shows that the Aryan cults do not find congenial soil among the aborigines. With the worship of Siva, in the Rajayogi sect, it was different. It was from this direction that a strong influence made itself felt in Thatiah's life.

A very old woman, bent with age, came to Thatiah's neighbourhood to visit her married daughter. This old woman, Bandikatla Veeramah, was a disciple of the Yogi Pothuluri Veerabramham. She must have been a spiritually-minded woman, and of strong personality. Thatiah and several others soon sat at her feet and learned of her.

The Yogi Veerabramham was one of the many reformers who rise up in India, influence thousands during several generations, and are then forgotten. This Yogi's influence seems to have been more far-reaching and more pure than that of many another. He has inspired thousands with a hope which in some of its features resembles the millennial hope in the mind of the Christian, who looks forward to a speedy second coming of the Christ. He taught that God is spirit, and must be worshipped in spirit. That which is not of the spirit was denounced by him. "Those who say 'Rama! Rama!' will fall away," he said, "because it is lip-service, and not of the spirit." In the book in which his disciples preserved much of his teaching, he calls upon the multitude to turn from wickedness and look forward to a coming incarnation. This expectation of a re-incarnation of the Deity was the central thought in his preaching, and he has so filled the minds of his followers with this hope that they look for its fulfilment in the immediate future.

The personal history of Veerabramham is clothed in much that is legendary. His father was a devotee of Siva; he himself, when a young man, saw a vision in the field, which invited him to a certain shrine, where he henceforth often held converse with the Deity. After the manner of the Yogi he entered his grave alive, and ordered to have the door closed. His chief disciple, Siddapa, who had been absent, came to the grave and called aloud to his master, for he had not given him the final initiation. With an invisible hand, the words which his master had to say to him were written on his tongue. He departed, and directed his preaching mainly against caste; and prophesied, in the name of his master that in the day when God again became incarnate caste would vanish and all men would be equal.

This was the teaching which Thatiah received from Bandikatla Veeramah. Her life was an illustration of her precepts. People of all castes came and went in her house, even Madigas, though she belonged to the goldsmith caste, and was, therefore, far above them.

The woman in whose house she and her daughter were living began to object to the custom of her tenants. She said, "All these people are coming and going. They may touch our cooking utensils, and thus spoil our caste. You can look for another house." Rather than ask her followers of low degree to stay away, Veeramah looked for another house. Her heart was large, she loved them all.

When she went away, she talked most lovingly to them: "You must be like the children of one mother, for you are the followers of one Guru. Be full of faith, don't go and sin. Strive without ceasing to earn salvation."

Thatiah had received his initiation as a Rajayogi Guru from Bandikatla Veeramah. For an hour every day he sat in meditation, his eyes closed, his fingers pressed over ears and nostrils, so that objects of sense might be completely shut out, and the soul might perceive the great, all-pervading Divine Being. He was much with the Rajayogi people, and seems to have been looked upon as a leader among them, because of his religious fervour.

In the Kanigiri Taluk, where Thatiah lived, the soil was dry and hard, and the Sudras had to dig wells in their fields to water the growing crops. In large buckets they brought the water to the surface, and these buckets were made of leather, and had to be made and kept in repair by the Madigas. Thatiah heard that much cattle was dying in the Godavery district, stung by a poisonous fly, and that, therefore, hides were cheap. He decided, with a kinsman, to go north on trade.

It was during his stay in that northern district that Thatiah first heard of the Christ. A Madiga, who was also bent on trade, told him of a Dora who was preaching this new religion. They decided to go and see him, and were kindly received. They went again. Thatiah said, "This religion is true. My soul is now satisfied." The Padre said, "You are going back to your home. Inquire from time to time, for soon a white teacher is coming to Ongole. Go to him; he will tell you more about this religion."

When Thatiah turned toward home, he was determined to break away from the old life and begin the new. He refused to bow before the village idols. He told the Rajayogi people that he was no longer one of them, that he had found something far better than they had to give. When they asked him which swami he was going to worship, he told them that he bowed to one, Jesus Christ, the Son of God, who had died for men. A Dora had told him, and another Dora was soon coming who would tell him more.

So bold a declaration from a man of the influence of Thatiah was not to be accepted with indifference. Some of the Madigas, who feared the demons and fiends of the village, predicted that their vengeance would smite them all, because of Thatiah's daring words. Nor were the Sudras pleased with his determination. His friends reasoned with him, "You are believing a God not of this country, but a new God. You are bringing new standards of living among us. Our old-time gods, Poleramah and Ankalamah, you no longer come to worship; you stay away when we beat the drums on their festal days. Don't you know that they will turn from us and curse us on your account?"

Thatiah was not a man to be abused. No one dared to insult him or ill-treat him. All the more keenly he felt the isolation when all withdrew from him. Those who had heretofore looked up to him as a spiritual leader now passed him by. Work that had been promised him by the Sudras was quietly withdrawn; the pay for work which he had done was not forthcoming.

But the grief that was deepest in all his sore trial came through the desertion of his wife Satyamah. She did not stand by him. Perhaps she was not greatly to blame; for she had not been with Thatiah when he opened his heart to the religion of Jesus Christ. He had told her all when he returned, but at the same time she saw him opposed on every hand. The change in him seemed like a wall between them; she felt that she was losing her husband, and when relatives and friends, who knew that Thatiah held her dear, told her that she must save him by sternly opposing him, she lent a willing ear.

Her former care for his comforts was turned to neglect. His food was often late or unsavoury, and sometimes he had to go hungry. When he wanted to drink there was no water. His remonstrances were met by reproaches from her. Finally he said to her: "By thus plunging me into all kinds of trouble, you cannot keep me here. I shall join the people of the Christian sect as soon as I can find them, and I shall eat with them." The strife was ended. When referring to this circumstance in later life, Thatiah said simply, "God in His great mercy changed her mind."

In all the forsaken condition of those days, Thatiah never forgot that a missionary was coming to Ongole. Could it be that he had already come? Satyamah agreed with him that it might be well to go and see.

Tired and footsore Thatiah came to the compound in Ongole, which was said to belong to the Nellore Missionary. In the midst of it was a little bungalow, but no white teacher living in it. As Thatiah went about the compound, he must have looked like a man who wanted something, for Gundla Pentiah saw him, and came out of his hut toward him, and asked, "Why did you come here?"

"I have come to look for the white teacher. Why is he not here?"

Pentiah was a Christian from Nellore, sent to Ongole to watch the compound and await the coming of the Missionary. He took Thatiah into his hut, and they talked it over. Pentiah grasped the situation; he sympathized with Thatiah, and he knew that there would be joy in the mission house at Nellore should a message be received that there was a man in Ongole, that spot of many prayers, who was hungering and thirsting after righteousness.

Pentiah knew of a way to do. He said, "Come with me to the house by the hillside, to a lady who is a friend of the Nellore Missionary. She will know what to do." They went, made a respectful salaam, and Pentiah, as spokesman said: "Ammah, this man, Thatiah, as he went north on trade, saw a missionary who told him that a white teacher would come to Ongole. He believes in Christ as God, and has come to see this teacher. As he does not find him here, he is very sad, and wants to know the reason of the delay. We have, therefore, come to make his request known to you."

The lady understood. She said to Thatiah: "I shall write to the Nellore Missionary. Be ready to come at any time when I send for you."

Not many days had passed when a cooley arrived in Thatiah's village, asking him to come to Ongole, for the Missionary had come. With his wife, Satyamah, he hastened on his way, barely taking needed rest as they walked the fifty miles. The joy when he saw the Nellore Missionary, and with him a younger man, who was soon to become the Ongole Missionary, is described by Thatiah as unspeakable. The older of the two men had been stoned in the bazaar of Ongole in the years gone by. But now, in the spot where his message had been spurned, he had a man before him who could not hear enough. A holy joy shone in the face of the one man; a yearning desire to hear more was in the face of the other as he sat hour after hour quenching his thirst.

Outcasts from their own community, Thatiah and his wife had made their way to Ongole. Received into the religious fellowship of the race that rules over India, they returned home. They could not have had more than a very dim conception of the fact that they were now counted among the hosts of men and women who represent the salt of the earth, yet they knew that their days of isolation were over. With a bundle of tracts and books on their shoulders, as many as they could carry, with the words of benediction from their white teachers ringing in their ears, and a new light in their countenances, they returned to their own village.

And now that ceaseless activity began that bore such abundant fruit. With untiring devotion Thatiah journeyed from village to village, his wife Satyamah always with him. The women loved Satyamah, and would gather about her and ask her whether she was not tired and thirsty after her journey, and take her away to refresh her. Late in life a mild insanity rendered her helpless. With a display of the same faithfulness which she had shown in accompanying her husband during twenty years, he now cared for her with a gentleness which called forth comment in the Madiga community. When her mind wandered, he took her by the hand, bade her sit down, and gave her to eat.

Thatiah stood like a granite pillar in the early days of the mission. He was a leader among his people, when the Madiga community was astir in discarding the old beliefs and accepting the new. He carried himself like a man of experience, of authority, in his humble sphere, to whose opinions deference should be paid. His bold features, measured gait, and a certain innate dignity, blended with a childlike humility, won for him the respect of all whom he addressed.

In his preaching he was not like other men, who had not pondered Rajayogi problems. He was wont to begin his discourses with some of the peculiar combinations of the Shastris. He would say, "The alphabet has five lines each way, thus also the body is composed of five elements. There is another five: two to hear, two to see, one to speak. But there is yet another five: the five wounds of Christ." By this time the interest of his hearers was aroused; it was a mode of proceeding congenial to the Hindu mind. In later years, when men trained in the Theological Seminary made their influence felt, critics arose, who said Thatiah might at last wheel into line. It was a species of the old strife between philosophy and theology. But Thatiah held his own. Hundreds believed in the Christ through his preaching. Spiritually-minded to an eminent degree, there was power in his words and his example.

In his old age Thatiah journeyed to Ongole once more. Slowly they brought him to his accustomed place on the platform of the chapel on Sunday morning. The Missionary stopped in his sermon to put him in his own chair. He saw the look of wonder on the faces of some of the younger generation, who knew little of the old days and its leaders. His heart was very tender toward the man who had never moved an inch from his God-appointed task, who had stood by his side in the days of small beginnings, in the days of calamity and of overwhelming responsibility.

He turned to the hundreds of listeners before him: "Do you want to know who this man is? I will tell you. When you get to heaven—and I hope you will all get there—you will see some one who looks radiant with light, far above you. You will almost need a telescope to see him distinctly, the distance between you and him will be so great. And you will ask some one, 'Who is that man clothed in exceeding brightness?' Then you will be told, 'That man is Bangarapu Thatiah from the Telugu country.' And you will strain your eyes to behold him."

There was a look of reverence on many a face as the Missionary proceeded with his sermon. A year later Thatiah's spirit took its flight.

SIX GURUS IN SUCCESSION

In the language of Western civilization Pullikuri Lukshmiah would have been called "a fast young man." He decked himself with earrings, finger-rings, bangles, belts, and various jewels, all of them conspicuous for glitter—not for their value. Red turbans and bright-coloured jackets lay in the box ready for use. He frequented places where there was dancing, singing, and festivity of every kind. Sin and lust grew apace, until a sense of disgust with the whole situation began to creep into his soul. He was weary of it all, and one day, he did not know from whence, the thought came: What if I should die?

At this juncture one of the wandering disciples of the Yogi Veerabramham came into the village and attracted Lukshmiah's attention. All his earnings were now spent on paying fees and giving gifts to this wandering Guru. He was bent on finding out something that might show him a way to salvation; he desired to secure a blissful state of the soul after death. But the days passed and he heard nothing definite, and one morning the Guru had taken his staff and wandered to the next place. But soon another came. Lukshmiah hovered around him. He did his share in giving the Guru to eat bountifully. He saw him partake of the intoxicating sarai freely, and then roll into a corner to sleep off the effects. After a few months he too went his way, and Lukshmiah found that he was none the wiser in knowledge.

Six Gurus were thus supported by Lukshmiah, wholly or in part, some for weeks, some for months. The rumour had spread in the Madiga community that he had lost interest in fine clothes and jewels, and was sitting at the feet of Rajayogi Gurus. Soon one after another of those who could claim some degree of kinship to him came to take advantage of this circumstance. They were his guests while they inquired of him concerning the hymns and mantras which he had heard, and the initiation through which he had passed. They were introduced to the Guru who happened to hold sway for the time being, and there was much inquiry and interest among them. Some of the friends came again and again. Bangarapu Thatiah, too, was sometimes among them, especially after Bandikatla Veeramah had gone away. A sense of cohesion was established among these men which lasted through many a year, for almost every member of this group became a strong force in Christian propaganda in the years that followed.

An honest search for truth is never wholly in vain. Lukshmiah and his friends had risen above the superstitions of the ordinary Madiga. They wanted something better, which shows that they had outgrown the beliefs of their childhood. Each individually tried what the abstractions of the Yogi could do to still the hunger of the soul. Friendship and a common interest had led them to meet and find out what the result on each might be. Each in his way had grown disheartened.

One after another of the friends went north to

trade in hides. Lukshmiah remained behind with the Guru Balli Somiah, who had been his instructor for two years. He lived in the village proper, with the Sudras, but his chief supporter was Lukshmiah. This meant a constant drain upon his resources. He was already deeply in debt. The Komati who had lent him money at different times demanded the interest, and it was compound interest. The hospitality freely offered to his friends and co-searchers in truth had cost him far beyond his means. They were gone, and there was a rumour that they were again banded together in the north, and that now they were investigating a religion which had come from the land of the English.

Lukshmiah decided to go north, and hoped that by the lucrative trade in hides he might cancel a part of his debt. But what should he do with the Guru Somiah, who showed no intention of leaving? It might prove dangerous to tell him that he could no longer support him, or to simply go away, leaving him in the lurch; for could he not pronounce a curse over him? But the presence and the sway of the Guru Somiah grew daily more irksome, till finally a way appeared to get rid of him. Lukshmiah knew that the Guru had a brother living in that northern district. He said to him: "Your disciples are all in the north, earning much money. I must go too; for my debts are very heavy. If you will come with me, you will find support." Thus the journey was undertaken.

Disappointment awaited the Guru Somiah when he reached the little settlement of his former followers. They wanted him no more. For the sake of old relationship they gave him food, but they omitted the sarai. He complained bitterly because the customary beverage was withheld. The friends talked it over and agreed to help Lukshmiah to get rid of his burden. They put together ten rupees and sent the Guru to his brother. Bangarapu Thatiah alone stood aloof, and said: "I shall give nothing. Send him away empty-handed as he came." But Pullikuri Lukshmiah rejoiced; for the presence of the Guru had hindered him greatly in making any progress in finding out what this new religion was.

To Lukshmiah, in the years that followed, the

mere mention of his former Gurus seemed like a breath of poison. It was the worthless character of the men that had obliterated anything of truth which might have lain hidden in their teaching. He says of those days: "I took hold of the feet of the disciples of Pothuluri Veerabramham and hoped to get salvation through them, but it was all in vain. What is the use of trusting in a bundle of wind? I thought I was doing pious deeds when I drank sarai with those Pothuluri people, but there was not the smell even of piety about me. However much husk you eat will hunger go?"

He had taken the lead among the friends in trying to get salvation in the Rajayogi sect. It had all come to nothing. He had wasted his substance on Gurus. In the investigations concerning the new religion he found the others in advance, and he must follow. One after another of the little colony of Madiga traders up in the Godavery district started on his homeward journey. He and his kinsman, Ragaviah, remained behind, intent on speculations that would bring financial gain.

Rumours had been brought to them that a missionary had come to Ongole, that everybody was talking about the new religion, and that some had said they would join this Christian sect. They longed for certain news, and were glad indeed when one day a friend and neighbour came from the old home on business, and visited them to tell them what had happened. The Ongole Missionary had come to Tallakondapaud and baptized twenty-eight, among them Lukshmiah's brother and his son, Ragaviah's son, and others of their friends and relatives.

After the visitor had left, the two men sat down together, sad at heart; they could hardly keep back the tears. Lukshmiah said: "The brother born after me and my own son are on the way to heaven before me. I cannot stay here longer." The next day they proceeded to hire sixteen bandies, to load one hundred hides on each, and to start for home. Eight bandy-loads were sold on the way, and with the remaining eight they arrived at home. Their sons, they found, were in Ongole in school, and they were glad that that which had been denied to them was being granted to their children. The Missionary had been informed of their return home, and a preacher was sent to tell them much about the religion of Christ that was new to them.

Lukshmiah was heavily in debt when he bade farewell to the last of the six Gurus of the Rajayogi sect on whom he had spent his substance. His former associates in the search for truth had become preachers, and were enduring the toil and enjoying the honours of their position. Lukshmiah held aloof. When questioned, he pointed to his debt. The fact was that the debt was an excuse, for as the years passed all was paid, with the exception, perhaps, of some of the compound interest. Lukshmiah was a man who preferred to be his own master. He did not want to become a link in the chain of organized preachers' work, but wanted to go about on his trade, make money, preach when and where he liked, and be answerable to no one.

Six years thus passed. The Missionary asked him, whenever he came to Ongole to the monthly meeting, whether the time had not come for him to cease going about on trade and to stay and do

God's work in earnest. He always replied he would come, but never came. Finally the scales were turned. It was a word from the Missionary that compelled him. Lukshmiah's son was leaving school and returning home for vacation. The Missionary told the young man to say to his father that the Dora sent salaams to him. He added: "When I call your father to work, he does not come; he runs about the country like a masterless dog." This word travelled over the country. Lukshmiah laughed at the time, and laughs to-day as he tells the story. The preachers all laughed; for they saw that Lukshmiah's undetermined position was well characterized by the Dora's words. But Lukshmiah's son said, "You must go"; and the father, still laughing, agreed that he must, but not just at present. What pleased Lukshmiah was that he had measured his strength with that of the Missionary, and in honest combat had been outdone. He was strong in holding aloof, but the Missionary was stronger in wheeling him right about and making him face his real position.

Soon after this the Missionary made an extensive tour through the Kanigiri Taluk. He saw that Lukshmiah, who joined the other preachers in accompanying him, was in fact the spiritual leader and pastor of a number of Christians in all the region round about his own village. Before they separated he had a talk with Lukshmiah and his wife. He said, "What would you like to do, Lukshmiah?" He replied, "I would like to engage in the Lord's service, but have a debt." The Missionary knew that this was all by way of excuse. He took a piece of paper that was lying on the table, tore it into small shreds, threw the handful of them over Lukshmiah, so that they flew to every corner of the tent, and said, "That is how your debt is gone." He gave him a friendly tap on the shoulder and sent him home.

On his way to his own village, Lukshmiah was stung in the face by a poisonous insect. Soon there was a painful swelling, and people said, "He will surely die; a Komati was thus stung and died." Lukshmiah was very anxious about this, and on the second day took the Bible to see whether he could not find something to comfort him at the prospect of a speedy death. He happened to turn to the chapters on the prophet Jonah's experience, and thought to himself that he too had fallen into trouble for refusing to preach as he was sent. He dictated a letter to the Dora: "I am coming, and will go to work." Two days later the swelling disappeared. He arose, visited a number of villages, preaching everywhere, and arrived in Ongole at the time of the monthly meeting.

The Dora saw him among the other preachers and smiled knowingly. "Have you come, Lukshmiah?"

'I have come."

THE SILENCE OF RAMASWAMI

As the Madigas of Yerrapallem came home from the fields at noon one day, they noticed some one sitting at a little distance from the village, as if taking rest from a journey. They said among themselves: "Who is this? Let us enquire his errand." One of them called the stranger to come under the large trees near their houses.

As he approached the group of men, he said: "My name is Bandaru Pulliah. I have come from Ongole, and have a way of salvation to make known to you. Will you hear it?" It was the noon hour, and the shade of the trees was pleasant. Why should they not hear something that was new and that excited curiosity?

There was a shrine of Ramaswami under one of the trees, where the Madigas of the village offered puja at stated intervals. Those who were ready to listen had grouped themselves in various attitudes, suggestive of ease and rest, but all at respectful distance from the shrine of the swami. Pulliah, to the astonishment of all, seated himself under the projecting roof of the shrine, and placed his feet, still covered with his sandals, against the wall of the shrine. They were a peaceful people before whom he thus displayed his contempt for the god, Ramaswami; they showed no sign of anger, but they feared for Pulliah. They had never dared go near the shrine with their sandals on their feet, lest the god smite them in wrath; but Pulliah smiled at their ejaculations of astonishment and fear. "Is the holy God in this shrine? Don't fear; no harm will come to me."

They watched him all that afternoon, and as they listened to this fearless man, who talked freely of Jesus Christ, his sandalled feet meantime boldly defiling the Ramaswami shrine, their respect for their god ebbed low, and they began to regard Pulliah in the light of an honoured guest.

When evening came, a little hesitation was felt with regard to asking him to eat with them; for he had told them frankly that Christians considered the practice of eating carrion both injurious and disgusting; yet they intended to care for his wants. The Madiga headman of the village asked him, therefore, whether he would come and eat with them of boiled rice and a little pepper sauce, or whether they should ask a Sudra to prepare his food for him. The latter course had to be taken whenever a Hindu Guru came to instruct them; but Pulliah declined this. He said, "Never mind; I'll eat with you."

They took him right in with them as one of themselves. The wife of the headman gave him to eat on a plate made of dried leaves sewn together, while she laid the food before her husband and sons in little earthenware bowls. The plate of leaves had never been used, and would be thrown away when Pulliah had ended his meal. This was considered a very genteel way of respecting the stranger's ideas of cleanliness.

That night the villagers sat in the white moonlight for hours listening to the stories of the divine life and death of the Christ, and to the explanations concerning the precepts of the new religion which Pulliah gave to them. They agreed that all he had told them seemed like a bright light as compared to the darkness in which they had thus far been living.

Pulliah was urged to remain with these kindly people for two days, and it happened while he was with them that their Guru came to look after the spiritual welfare of his followers, and at the same time after his own material interests. He generally sat down and said: "Cut a fowl! Make rice and curry! Bring sarai!" The lads of the family would press his limbs, saying, "The Guru is tired," and hope in this way to receive divine reward.

But this time the reception given to the Guru lacked that element of devout reverence for his person to which he was accustomed. The villagers poured water and washed his feet, but they omitted to catch it again in bowls, and to drink it in the hope of eternal reward. The Guru met with a quiet air of resistance when,

A HINDU GURU.

[Page 144.

as usual, he demanded fowls and intoxicating drink for his meal. As he sat under the tree no one asked for his mantras, but, instead, he heard how Pulliah told the villagers that, if they wanted to become Christians, they must have their juttus cut off, for no Christian could have a lock of hair growing on his head to afford a dwelling-place for a swami. Pulliah carried a pair of scissors ever in his pocket; for hundreds of juttus was he called upon to cut off in his wanderings. The men of the village bent their heads and said, "Cut them off." While all were thus engaged, and even the young boys came and asked to be shorn of their top-knots, the Guru arose. He looked neither to the right nor to the left; he made salaam to no one; he went away and never returned.

It was decidedly in Pulliah's favour as he went about, gaining access to many a Madiga household, that he was generally considered well-connected by family relationship. The Madigas manifest their clannish spirit by seeking to establish new relationships by intermarriage of families, and such connections, though often remote, are cherished. Many a door was opened to Pulliah because his family had had an interest in a marriage that had at some time been celebrated between a man of one family and a girl of another.

Another circumstance in his favour was the fact that he had been much with the Rajayogi people in his boyhood. He was familiar with their phraseology, their customs and beliefs; in short, he spoke their language, and was, therefore, recognised as one of them wherever he went. Pulliah was related to Bangarapu Thatiah and other men who for a time took an interest in the Rajayogi sect. In his wanderings he sought, therefore, first of all for Rajayogi people; for they had gone beyond the swamis of the Madiga village, and had at least the desire to know and see the one God, whom they had been taught to worship. It was a joyful mission to tell such seekers that God had become incarnate in the man Jesus Christ.

When Pulliah left Yerrapallem, the heads of the several leading families of the village assured him that idol-worship would from henceforth be stopped, that Sunday should be a day of rest, and that no carrion should be brought into the village. They promised to pray to Jesus Christ, on their knees, as they had seen him do. Some months passed; Pulliah came often. Two of the older men began to ask, "Why should we not be baptized?" Pulliah offered to take them with him to Ongole at the time of the monthly meeting, and with a staff in their hands and a little bundle of cooked rice on their shoulders they began their journey of forty miles.

There were others who were journeying on the same road. Here and there they were joined by fellow-travellers. If the little company stopped at some Madiga hamlet by the road, to ask for water to drink, they had to give an account of their motives for undertaking this journey. They met Yettis on the way, who carried the news far and near that more Madigas were on the way to Ongole. Toward evening of the third day they entered the mission compound. Groups of men and women were sitting around the little fires kindled under pots of rice, waiting till the women should announce that it had cooked enough. There was much talking, much questioning, much interchange of experience. There was a hospitable, brotherly spirit, too, as they cared for each other's wants.

The preachers took an interest in the experience of the two men from Yerrapallem. The Missionary talked with them. They felt some hesitation when they saw his white face, for they had never before seen a Dora. He spread mats on the floor and asked them to sit down, since they were unaccustomed to chairs. And then the Dorasani came and put plantains into the hands of her little children to take to these visitors, and she talked with them. Their fears soon went.

One of them was received for baptism; concerning the second, Papiah, a serious obstacle arose in the way. He had two wives, and was, therefore, put off. The men were astonished, for it had not entered their minds that this might be an objection. They said to themselves: "We did not know that this was sin. We Hindus do such things. But if it is not God's will, then it must be stopped."

It was an arrangement which had been made

by Papiah's mother. Her niece, whose husband had deserted her, was destitute, and the old mother saw no reason why she should not be brought into Papiah's house as a second wife, for thus she would be provided with a home. The first wife was made unhappy by this arrangement; but she had only a daughter, no son, and, therefore, was not given a voice in the matter. She was deeply angry with her husband, and refused to be on friendly terms with the new wife; but there was no help for her: she had to bear the ills of her new position in silence, lest she should be harshly treated, or even beaten.

When the travellers returned from Ongole, the matter was thoroughly discussed in the village. The old mother was angry, and wanted to know who had ever heard that a man should not have two wives. The preachers came and went during the weeks that followed, and tried to explain matters to those who enquired for the reason why Papiah should have been refused baptism. They spoke of Adam and Eve, that God gave to Adam only one wife; they insisted that, according to the teachings of the New Testament, the man and both the women would lose the salvation of their souls. The preachers were themselves men who until recently had not been aware of the religious and ethical transgression involved in the practice of polygamy. The Madigas, among whom the standard of social morality is, in some of its aspects, very low, were thus suddenly brought face to face with the purer conceptions of married life as upheld by Christian civilization.

After the matter had been thoroughly discussed by all the family, and those who objected to the introduction of ideas contrary to the customs of Indian village life had been silenced, a way was found out of the difficulty. The second wife had relatives in the village, who offered her a home with them. She had a child, but it was a girl; had it been a boy, her fate might have been different. There had been no marriage ceremony; she, therefore, went as she had come. Her child died soon after, and she went to live with another man, again without ceremony. The first and only legitimate wife of Papiah now had peace once more.

There was a social as well as a religious upheaval wherever Christianity entered the Madiga community. The pure precepts of the new religion were taken up by one family after another. The juttu was cut off as the outward sign of a religious change. But when a man sat apart at meal-time because carrion was boiling in the pot, it was regarded as the signal of a change of a social nature. "Do you see him? He will not eat! He, too, is going to that Ongole religion!" Sometimes persecution within the family circle followed, and there were sad and weary days and months for the heretic.

When Christian families had visitors who still continued the old customs, they gave them to eat as much as they wanted, but refused to let them touch the earthen plates of the family. Their food was put on old plates that could be thrown away when they had finished. They gave them to drink from the brass cup, because it could afterwards be scoured with sand. They said: "We turn sick when you touch our food. You are unclean." Instead of being ostracized, they were the ones who ostracized the others.

Many a man and a woman who was deaf to

spiritual advice first leant an ear because he was despised by the family on account of his noisome food. Legends and traditions spoke of the curse pronounced over the Madigas, that they should be carrion-eaters. Nothing had had power to lift the curse until now it was fought in Christian family-centres. Argument was unnecessary. Did not many among them succumb tò disease, the direct consequence of their loathsome food? Did not the suffering of the children in the villages bear evidence of the filthy habits of their parents?

A new day had dawned. The gospel of cleanliness had entered in. When filth departs, ignorance must go with it. Only a few years after the day when Pulliah had fearlessly placed his sandalled feet upon the shrine of Ramaswami, a teacher came from Ongole to settle in the village Yerrapallem. Willing hands offered to raise the mud walls of the little school-house. Each household contributed to the thatch for the roof. The beam, too, was finally paid for, and made ready by the village carpenter.

As for the site of the school-house, it was decided that the shrine of Ramaswami must yield its place. The Sudras shook their heads in doubt, but when several preachers came to help make room for the school-house, the courage of the Christians rose high. They took the pick-axe and shovel. The walls of the shrine fell. A little snake that lay in a crevice was disturbed. It raised its head and hissed but once before the death-blow fell. But Ramaswami must have been afar off He gave no sign of wrath.

FROM NASRIAH TO CHRIST

Nasriah the Reformer

Longing to See God

His Mother's Curse

NASRIAH THE REFORMER

It happened again and again that men and women told me, "Before I became a Christian I belonged to the Nasriah sect."

I naturally enquired what this sect was.

"The Gurus of the Nasriah sect came to us and said, 'Don't steal, don't worship idols, don't drink sarai.' It was a good religion, for they taught us that there is only one God."

"Did many Madigas belong to it?"

The answers were vague. One man said there were at least one hundred. The next man said there must have been one thousand. The third man said, "How can I know?"

I asked many questions. Who was this Nasriah? When did he live? Where in the multiplicity of Hindu cults was his teaching to be classed? I found a man who said he had been in Tiprantakamu at the annual feast of the Nasriah sect. Another said he had seen Sundramah, the last surviving disciple of Nasriah.

Finally I heard of a man, a Madiga, who was said to have seen Nasriah himself. I sent for him. He came—a stern old man, with Roman nose and shaggy brows. "Did you, yourself, see Nasriah?"

He laid five finger-tips in each eye; he bent towards me, and the attitude and tenseness of his body emphasized his words: "With these eyes I saw Nasriah."

Thus I had Nasriah placed as to time. This man was seventy years old, at most seventy-five. His father had been carried away with the religious movement produced by Nasriah, and had taken him, as a little boy, to Tiprantakamu. There the lad had seen Nasriah, a few years before his death, which must have occurred about the year 1825.

I hoped to hear something about the personality of the remarkable man, Nasriah, whose influence was so wide-spread, even after many years. But the stern old man before me could tell me nothing about the man, though he was ready to tell me much about the sect which bears his name. For years he was an initiated Guru of that sect. I gathered from him all he could tell me, but the more I heard the more I desired to know who this Nasriah was. I sent word in several directions whether there was any man living who remembered hearing his father tell any story about the Guru Nasriah. Thus a Mohammedan was discovered whose father had been an initiated disciple of Nasriah, and had often told him the story of the way in which Nasriah became so great a Guru. He himself had seen him when a young boy. He was now an old man, and the story which he told is characteristic of the religious life of India.

There lived, a hundred years ago, a Mohammedan of the Syed sect, who was a wealthy trader. He owned several ships, and often went on long voyages. On one of his voyages, Galep Sherif—for such was his name—met with a Guru whose teaching attracted him. He asked for instruction, and then proceeded to obey his teacher implicitly. His lucrative business was given up. In the Baputla Taluk he built himself a temple, where he dwelt, and many came to hear his teaching. His main doctrine was that there is only one God.

The Rajah of Narsaravapetta heard of Galep Sherif and the supernatural power which he possessed to work miraculous deeds. He sent his messenger to invite the Guru to his palace, intimating that he had some inclination to become his disciple. Galep Sherif came. He waited a day or two, but the Rajah delayed to summon him to his presence. Not willing to wait longer, he arose and started on his homeward journey.

Now the Rajah had an attendant, Nasr Mahomed by name, of the Shaik sect, who was deeply interested in this Guru. He followed him as he left the palace, fell at his feet, and begged to be instructed as his disciple. The Guru demanded an initiation fee of four hundred rupees. So intent was Nasr Mahomed on receiving the desired instruction that he promised the fee, though he knew he had nothing wherewith to pay it. After he had been taught even the power to perform miracles, the day approached when he must pay the promised fee. Nasr Mahomed rose up and fled. He reached Tiprantakamu, where there was a Hindu temple. The attendants at the temple and the worshippers who came listened to his teaching, and the number of his followers increased daily.

Galep Sherif became aware of the hiding-place of his disciple, Nasr Mahomed, and appeared in person at the temple to demand the promised fee. There was deliberation among the followers of Nasr Mahomed. They said: "He is a great Guru. Let us pay his debt, and then let us build him a temple. He will stay among us, and we shall earn salvation." Galep Sherif received his fee and went his way. A large temple was built, and ere long the influence of the new Guru was felt far and near. The common people gave to the Mohammedan name *Nasr* the Telugu ending, and thus the sect became known as the Nasriah sect.

And what was the creed of Nasriah? By birth he was a Mohammedan, yet I never heard that he or his followers mentioned Mohammed, the prophet. The Guru with whom Galep Sherif came in contact on his voyage must have been a Yogi. The teaching of Nasriah is largely Yogi doctrine. In fact, his followers called themselves Rajayogi people. The Mohammedan and the Yogi alike assert that there is one God.

The following instructions for devotion, given by Nasriah, coincide with Yogi doctrine: "Concentrate your mind. Put away all secret thoughts. Turn the eye upward. Forget the existence of the body. Let the sight turn towards the coil of hair on top of the head (as worn by sanyasis). Gaze with firm mind. The following will appear: Light, angelic spirits, sacred rivers and places, also Rishis, the sun and moon, lightning, thunder, fire, water, sound will fill the heavens, the earth will appear as if it were an egg, Brahma will be seen, all as if one."

Nasriah made disciples and sent them out to preach. He made no distinction of either caste or sex. Women as well as men passed through the initiatory rites, and then went forth to make converts. I enquired about these rites, but came upon a solid wall of silence every time. The most that any one told me was that something was whispered into their ear which must never be passed on to any one who was not in turn found worthy to receive initiation.

During the life-time of Nasriah his disciples feared to do what he had forbidden. He rebuked them when he found that sarai and bhang were used by them. He frowned on caste distinction. He was a man whose righteous indignation could overpower him. Even those who could not tell me who Nasriah was could tell of his act of vengeance when he shed blood to mark his hatred of lust. He heard one day the cry of one of his female disciples who was being insulted and injured. He caught the evil-doer, and stabbed him in the heart. Nothing was done to him, for, though he was imprisoned, none could hold him. The common people saw him pass through the prison walls and walk about in the bazaar while the keepers stood at the prison door. Such were the tales told of Nasriah, and they explain much of the powerful hold which he had upon the people.

After his death the sect became corrupt. His disciples said it could do no harm to worship idols. In their ethical precepts they grew lax. Why should not a man steal if he could do so without exposure? It was irksome to abstain from sarai and bhang. It seems that even the most revolting forms of Sakti-worship entered the sect.

I doubt whether the separate temple for the Madigas at Tiprantakamu was built during the life-time of Nasriah. He would not have permitted such emphasis on caste-distinction. One of his earliest converts seems to have been a Madiga, who was made a Guru, and was sent out to convert his people. To belong to the Nasriah sect meant advancement to the Madigas. They realized that the theism of Nasriah was better than the polytheism of their village cults. One man said to me: "A Yogi first told me that I am of sinful nature, and must seek to earn salvation. I never before had thought of myself in that way." Another man said: "Beside our own village gods, I worshipped the idols of Vishnu. But when the Rajayogi people came and told me that there is one God, and that idols are useless, I believed them. It was much better than anything I had before heard." It raised the Madigas in the social scale, too, to belong to the Nasriah sect, for when they went to Tiprantakamu in the autumn of the year to the annual feast, they

IDOL WORSHIP.

[*Page* 161.

stood in a line with people of all castes and classes.

Whole families went to the feast together. They took with them a goat, fowls, rice, tamarind, and the various spices used for curry. All these they delivered to Sundramah, as they bowed low before her with special reverence, for she was the last of the band of disciples who gathered around Nasriah. They laid flowers on the grave of Nasriah, and worshipped there. Sundramah took all that was brought, and passed it on for the general cooking. The food for all who came, regardless of caste, was boiled in one pot, and when it was time to eat, all sat down and ate together. But the Madigas sat a little to one side. Not even in the Nasriah sect would the Sudra sit side by side with the Madiga and eat with him.

When the movement toward Christianity began among the Madigas, the men and women who had sought salvation in the Nasriah sect were among the first to open their hearts to the divine life that is in Christ. The followers of Nasriah became the disciples of Christ. At Tiprantakamu it was said,

"The Madigas are leaving us." Some shrugged their shoulders. "What can we do to hold them? They are following a new religion." Others said, "Let them go." And thus the Nasriah sect became to many a man as the memory of a stepping-stone to something higher.

LONGING TO SEE GOD

The fame of the Ulluri family was spread abroad in the land, not for their wealth, nor for leadership in great and noble deeds, but because they were devout. They had given to their Guru, Poliah, a cow worth sixteen rupees. This was considered a very noble gift to offer to a Guru, and established the reputation of the family for religious devotion.

Chinnapudy Poliah, though wholly illiterate, seems to have been a man possessed of a severe type of earnestness, that distinguished him from others, and supported his claim to being a Guru. He was a man who indulged in deep meditation, and was a dreamer of dreams. One day he reasoned in this wise: "The swami at Kottapakonda and the swamis at other places where people go to worship were all made by men. Now who made these men? Who made earth and heaven? Must I die without seeing God?" His father was a follower of Nasriah. It was one of the earliest recollections of Poliah that his father took him to Tiprantakamu to see Nasriah. The lad never forgot the man who lived in poverty, like a sanyasi, ever ready to talk with any one of his chief doctrine—that there is only one God. Nasriah planted antagonism to idol-worship into the mind of the boy, and with it a restless desire to see God.

In his ministrations to the Ulluri family the Guru, Poliah, knew how to clothe his ignorance round about with a mantle of profound reverence. There were hymns and mantras which he taught them. He had caught a word here and there of the philosophy of the Rajayogi people, and gave a glimpse of his wisdom on special occasions to his followers; but as soon as he found himself going beyond his depth, he withdrew with that air of mystery which is so fascinating to simple-minded people. He would promise to tell them more next time, and thus kept them ever filled with curiosity, and on the alert, wondering what he would tell them when he came again.

One of the promises which Poliah was ever holding out to his followers was that they should see God. Now the aged father of the family had a great desire to see God. He was respected by all, and his sons began to consider the matter in earnest. They talked with Poliah, who demanded fifteen rupees as a fee. They thought this was too much. He waxed eloquent in describing the severe test which he had to undergo before he acquired the knowledge of the mystic formulæ. He pointed out that the whole family would without doubt obtain salvation if one of their number succeeded through his efforts in seeing God. Finally, Poliah agreed to be satisfied with eleven rupees, and the night was decided upon when the attempt should be made.

Ten men and women, who had faith, and were filled with the desire to see God, sat together at midnight in the house of the Ulluri family. Two little oil-lamps stood in niches in the wall, shedding a dim light on the scene. The Guru sat in the centre, his followers in a circle around him. He sang hymns and invocations of the Nasriah sect, and then proceeded to draw mystic circles, saying mantras as [he drew them. His demeanour inspired awe, and his followers held their breath and feared to move.

At last the decisive moment had come. He motioned to all to withdraw, leaving only the aged father within. More mantras were said, more mystic figures were drawn, and then the father of the Ulluri family laid his fingers against his eyes, ears, and nostrils, as Poliah had previously instructed him to do. He understood, too, that he was thus to shut off all connection with the outer world, and to perceive God with an inner sense.

A little time elapsed, and then Poliah asked, in an awed whisper, whether he saw anything.

"All looks red and green, and in it I see something as if it were the picture of a man."

"It is God," said Poliah; "you have seen Him."

Dazed and full of wonder, the old man joined his children without. He thought it over many a day, as he sat in the shade of the house, his grandchildren playing around him. Many came and went, and he had to tell them how it all seemed to him. It was a source of deep satisfaction to the good old man, and his sons did not begrudge the money it cost them.

Some years had passed when, one day, Wasipogu Bassiah came to Maduluri to get the tools with which he did his leather-work sharpened. He was a friend of the Ulluri family, and went to them for a visit before he returned to his home, three miles distant. While they were talking of this and that, he asked whether they had heard of the new religion, which a Dora had brought to Ongole, and which was said to be a good religion. They had not, but asked for further information. Bassiah could not satisfy them; he had only heard that those who believe in this religion are saved through one, Jesus Christ, that He must be worshipped, and no other swamis whatsoever beside Him. Moreover, a Yetti had told him that he knew several Madigas who had joined this new sect, and they did no work on Sunday, nor would they allow carrion to be brought into their village.

Bassiah went home. Near his house he found

a man sitting under a tree, evidently resting after a journey. He had enquired for the Madiga headman of the village, and was told he would soon come. As headman it was Bassiah's duty to receive strangers, to enquire after their errands, and lend assistance if there was an appeal to him in his official capacity. Now when Bassiah heard that the man before him, Baddepudy Kanniah, was a follower of the sect which worships Jesus Christ, he was glad. He cared for his wants; in fact, he took charge of Kanniah. The tribal system of the Indian village community thus lent itself as a vehicle to Christian propaganda. Next day they went to Maduluri, and were well received as guests. They were asked to sit on a raised seat, made of stone, and as the villagers gathered around, Bassiah told them why Kanniah had come to them, and they agreed that it would be well to listen to all he had to say.

Little was said at the time, but after their visitors were gone some among the villagers expressed an opinion that it would be well to hear more about this religion, and proposed that they extend an invitation to come again in the evening, to eat with them, and then to talk more. This was done. Two men were sent to extend the invitation of the villagers, which was accepted. Kanniah had the best of opportunities that night. All were intent on hearing; the little children were asleep, and only the occasional barking of the village dogs broke the silence of the night. The hearts of the listeners were stirred within them when they heard the story of the death of Christ; and then, when Kanniah prayed after the manner of the Christian, who does not hesitate to make his thoughts known to his Father who is in heaven, they felt that they had never known anything like this before, and they said among themselves in the days that followed: "Why should we go on as heretofore? There is no salvation in all that we have been doing."

As the younger men of the Ulluri family were discussing the new religion with several young kinsmen, who had come from a little distance, as soon as they heard from a passing Yetti that strange things were taking place in Maduluri, the aged father of the Ulluri family advised them to take time to consider. He asked them to remember that they had not been without religious zeal heretofore. Had not the whole family on one occasion journeyed to the grave of Nasriah at Tiprantakamu, with goodly offerings of rice and a goat? Did they not lay garlands on the grave, singing appropriate hymns? Had they not given to the Guru Poliah a cow, in return for his ministrations? And, above all, had not he, their father, at midnight some years ago, been allowed to see God?

Moreover, this Madiga patriarch had a daughter, Ukkamah, whom he held dear, with a peculiar love and respect. When about ten years old she became a widow. In her infancy, in imitation of the customs of the Aryan Hindu, her parents had married her to a young lad of a family well known to them. The second ceremony, when she would be led as a bride to his house, had not been performed. And now, like the Brahmin widow, this little Madiga maid was never to marry, not because it would have been contrary to Madiga usage, but because it was thought well to follow the example of the twice-born Brahmins.

As the years passed, Ukkamah took comfort

in the religious rites taught by the disciples of Nasriah. Her parents encouraged her in singing the hymns of that sect, accompanying herself on the cithara. It came about gradually, after she was forty years of age, that she was asked to come to villages here and there and sing and play. She was treated with much respect. People said, "She is not like other women. She serves God." After a time a cousin also lost her husband, and the two women henceforth went about together. They were not allowed to go away from any village where they had sung empty-handed. Money accumulated in their hands; they laid some of it as an offering on the shrine of Nasriah. Ukkamah gave a part of hers toward the support of her parents.

Ukkamah was now at a distant village, and her father insisted that, before any decisive step was taken, her opinion must be asked, for had she not more piety than any one else in the family? Condiah, the eldest son, was restless during the days that followed. Finally, he said: "Ukkamah is not coming. I shall go to her." Two days he journeyed. There was welcome in his sister's eyes when she saw him. "Is it well with all at home?" was her first question. She told the village people that her brother had come, and all gathered with a friendly curiosity, and the wife of the Madiga headman brought buttermilk in a brass vessel, that he might drink and be refreshed.

When brother and sister sat down to talk, Condiah soon found that he had no opposition to face. Ukkamah said: "I have heard of this religion. We said in the Nasriah sect that there is one God. This was right; but we did wrong, because we continued to worship idols. It is well that you have the desire to go to Ongole. Do not wait for me. Go at once. Soon I shall return home, and then I, too, shall make known my faith in Jesus Christ." These were Ukkamah's words; and as Condiah repeated them after his arrival at home, all were satisfied that the time had come when they should break away from the old, and enter upon the new life.

The Ulluri family was sufficiently prominent to make the change in their various relations a matter of comment. The Sudras were much displeased with them. Never before had the Ulluri family refused to come to work, as they now did, when called on the Sunday. The number of Christians was rapidly increasing, and all showed this same spirit of insubordination, which the Sudras had never before known among their serfs. "Let us teach them," they said.

It was harvest time, and since some of the Christians had helped to plough and till the soil, it was their right, according to ancient custom, to receive their share of the grain. To enforce a lesson, the Sudras thrashed their grain on Sundays, and the Christians, who showed their moral courage in staying away, thus incurred considerable loss.

On a Sunday the Sudras were all out on the fields at work; only a few had remained behind in the village. The old mother of the Munsiff made a fire to boil a little milk. While away for a few minutes, the fire touched a basket of bran standing near, which soon burned lustily, and, before the people could be called from the fields, ten of the houses were destroyed by fire. All the grain that had been gathered on those

Sundays, to spite the Christians, was burned. The old mother ran away to hide herself for half a day, and when she again appeared, half distracted, she wailed, "God sent it as a punishment!" She had been specially harsh in her attitude toward the Christians, and that she should have been the cause of so much loss seemed to all a judgment direct from God. The strife was now ended. Henceforth the Sudras attended to small jobs on Sunday, and did their important work when the Christians could join them.

The vexation of the Sudras was again roused when they prepared a feast to one of the village matris, and sent for the Madigas to beat the drums and dance before the idol. It was one of the duties which they owed to the community on the ancient system of mutual service. But now they sent word that they could not come.

A message came back to them: "Then you stay by yourselves, and we stay by ourselves. You need not serve us any more. We do not want you."

The Sudras thought it would be an easy matter

to supply the places, but found themselves mistaken. Those who were not already Christians had a sense of clannish honour, and refused to come into work that had been taken from others of their tribe. Only a few worthless fellows came. The Sudras, therefore, thought best to make peace.

The Ulluri family was related to a number of other family groups, and it soon became known among them all that the Guru, Poliah, had been advised to become a Christian, as the only way in which he could obtain salvation. But some of the more distant branches of the family circle did not grasp the significance of the change. They thought a change of Gurus had taken place but that the ancient cults of the Madigas could not thereby be touched.

It happened one day that a messenger from a branch of the family, living ten miles away, brought an invitation to attend a feast to Perantalu. Several of the men of the family said: "We are Christians. What have we to do with Perantalu?"

Others said, "Let us go and tell them what we think of their markings on the wall."

They went, and the unsuspecting hosts were overcome by the indignant demand that the markings be scratched from the wall, or their guests would not touch a morsel of the rice and curry which had been prepared.

One of them meekly remarked: "Heretofore it made no difference which sect any one joined, he could yet worship Perantalu. Is it then different with Christianity?"

In the midst of argument and dispute some one took his sandals and offered to scrape the yellow saffron and red dots of Perantalu off the wall. It was done. Harmony was restored. The feast was enjoyed without being first offered to the departed female ancestress of the family, for whom the markings had been made.

"What good thing can she do for us? What evil will she ward off? It is God's blessing that we want," said one of the guests.

Another branch of the family were preparing for the annual feast to Nagarpamah. They worshipped Naga, the hooded serpent, personified as a woman, a combination of Sakti worship and the ancient serpent-worship. The huge ant-hills out in the fields, in which the white ants have their nests, are often the abodes of snakes, that coil in and out of the passages dug by the ants, and feed on the larvæ. Once a year a feast is made to Nagarpamah, when her supposed abode is painted with saffron and red dots. Water is poured over the ant-hill to induce Nagarpamah to grant plentiful harvest; cooked rice is placed in front of it, and milk is poured into the passages. Puja is then made, and, whether there is any trace of a snake in the ant-hill or not, the worshippers go away satisfied to enjoy their own feast, for they believe that Nagarpamah is aware of the worship that has been offered her.

After hearing of the summary proceedings with the markings of Perantalu, it was thought best to put off the annual feast to Nagarpamah. In fact, it was never held, for Christianity spread so rapidly it carried all before it.

There were Ellama worshippers in the family who were ashamed to have anything to do with the Ellama-house, and the pot with the emblematical shells hung from the roof within. The

Matangi of that region looked on with a displeasure which she did not try to conceal.

Schools were started. The brightest lads were sent to Ongole to study, and the men and women who sought for salvation in the Nasriah sect were singled out one after another to do valiant service at important centres of the movement of the Madigas toward Christianity.

HIS MOTHER'S CURSE

The young man, Kommu Puniah, wanted to make sure, before he started on his journey north, to trade in hides, that when he returned he might wed the maiden, Subbamah. She was a comely girl, about thirteen years old, and, as she was a distant relative, he had often seen her, but of late years he had not dared to speak to her, for such was not the custom.

He had spoken to her family concerning her, and they had agreed to the marriage. But he loved Subbamah, and one day, as he stood talking with her grandmother, he knew that Subbamah was behind the door, listening to every word. He said: "I shall be gone one year, and when I return I shall have rupees in my hands. Do not let Subbamah marry any one while I am gone." The old grandmother replied, "When you return, we shall give her to you as a wife." Something moved behind the door, and Puniah knew that Subbamah had put her hand up to her face, and that she was pleased.

Not one year, but five years, Puniah stayed in that northern district, and never did he hear of a Madiga returning home with his cart-loads of hides but he sent word to Subbamah's grandmother that he was doing well, and would soon come home to wed Subbamah.

Puniah belonged to the Nasriah sect, and so did his kinsman, Seshiah, who was with him in the north. A Madiga, Darla Yelliah, a trader in hides, who made frequent journeys back and forth, came to them once in six months to buy of them the hides which they had traded from the Sudras. This man, Yelliah, was a Christian and the three men began to discuss their religious beliefs, after they had settled their trade in hides. Yelliah sang a Christian hymn, and the other two men sang a Nasriah hymn, but asked to be taught the Christian hymn.

Yelliah said they ought to let all the forms and customs of the Nasriah sect go, and pray to the true God. They wanted to know how this was done. It happened that they were on the bank of a river, on the way to some distant village. Yelliah took a cloth which hung over his shoulder, and spread it on the ground. He told his companions to kneel with him, and to listen, for he was going to talk with his God, who was his Father. Before he left them that day, Yelliah taught them the ten commandments. They said after he was gone, "We can continue to sing Nasriah hymns, but it would be well to pray as Yelliah did."

Whenever Yelliah passed that way he told them more, and after a time they said, "We will stop drinking sarai and eating carrion." But the Malas, with whom they had made a contract for hides, were displeased. They said: "You are not living like Madigas. You do not eat carrion. You are Christians." They refused to fulfil their part of the contract, and as Puniah had nothing in his hands by way of proof, he lost all he had advanced. After that he bought hides outright, though it was not as lucrative as by contract.

Puniah returned home, married and settled, and was prosperous. He found a man who could read a little, and asked him to teach him. Through him he heard that a Dora had come to Ongole, and decided to go and see. He took a load of goat-skins and journeyed to Ongole to sell them. As he entered the mission compound he met Pentiah, and sat down to have a talk with him under the trees. He was interested in the pretty booklets which Pentiah was selling. Books always had an attraction for Puniah. Years after, when he was an ordained preacher, he had accumulated a library of Telugu tracts and books, as many as were to be had. The fewness of the books gave evidence of the paucity of Christian Telugu literature. But Puniah was proud of his library, till one day, before any one observed it, the white ants came and ate it all. Later he bought of a mission family, for a few rupees, a "meat-safe," made of teak-wood, which the white ants cannot eat, and, as he explained to me, "iron windows all around," by which I understood wire-netting. In this piece of furniture, made to keep food from flies and insects and beetles, Puniah felt that his new library would be safe. With his love for books even then Puniah readily agreed to take a number of tracts away with him, to sell them for Pentiah in the villages where he went to trade in hides. Before he left, the two men went to the bungalow, and Pentiah introduced Puniah to the Dora as a man who is living like a Christian and is willing to sell tracts. The Dora invited him to come to Ongole to school, and he said he would come.

This invitation was repeated several times as Puniah came and went on trade. He agreed every time that he would come, but the trading instincts were strong within him; he hesitated because he had plans for accumulating rupees. One day he came with a bandy-load of goat-skins to Ongole, and, as usual, went to see the Dora.

He said, "How are you, Puniah?"

With the affirmative nod of the head common among the Telugus, Puniah said, "I am well."

"How much money did you get this time?"

"I got thirty rupees;" and he proudly rolled the silver out of the red cloth which he had tied tightly around his waist.

The Dora held out his hand and took them, and said: "This is the fine for your wavering words.

Four times you have told me you are coming to school, and you have not done it. Salaam." And the Dora went into the bungalow.

But Puniah did not go. He stood outside and watched the Dora walking about inside. Twice he came to the door and asked, "Why do you not go?"

"I want my money."

Finally, the Dora called him, took him by the shoulder, gave him a kindly shake which almost took the young man off his feet, but pleased him exceedingly. "Here is your money. Will you come to school?"

"I will come."

But the Dora called his preacher, and said: "Jonathan, this young man lied to me four times. He now says he will come to school. If he does not come—you are witness—you must deliver him over to me. Write down his name." Jonathan wrote his name, and he went home.

After this Puniah was restless. He sold his cattle, paid his debts, and when everything was ready, and he was planning to start for Ongole, his wife, Subbamah, said, "I will not go." Now,

Subbamah was a good-looking young woman, and she liked to adorn herself with beads around her neck and bangles on her arms. When they were married the Madiga Dasiri had, according to custom, taken the talibottu from a pile of rice and handed it to Puniah to tie around Subbamah's neck, in the presence of all their relatives, as the sign of marriage. The talibottu was of the size of a coin, very thin, but made of gold. Her other ornaments had very little of gold or silver in their composition, but they looked well.

It seems in the early days, when the first converts among the women saw that the Dorasani did not wear bangles or beads, they thought it was part of the Christian religion to do without these ornaments. Bangarapu Thatiah's wife, Satyamah, broke her bangles, and wherever she and her husband went in those days it was remarked that when they preached in the Rajayogi sect they wore silver rings, but now they had nothing.

The glass bangles which the women wear are not merely ornaments: they show that the wearer is not a widow. Among the Brahmins, when a man dies his relatives take away from his widow all the jewels she wears. Sometimes they are torn from her cruelly. I think it must be in imitation of this custom among the twice-born Aryans that the Madigas take the widow to the new-made grave of her husband and let the Madiga Dasiri with a stick break the glass bangles on her arm, so that the pieces fall upon the ground.

It happened during the early years of the Mission that the wife of one of the preachers went to a village where she was well known, her arm bare of the customary glass bangles. "Go away," said the women to her; "we do not want your God. When you were here before, your husband was living. Now look at your arm—your bangles are gone. What has your new God done for you?" After this, it seems, the Missionary and his wife told the women to keep their bangles, because they saw that a social custom was involved, with which it was not well to interfere.

Puniah's wife, Subbamah, had evidently heard of this, and she said she did not want to go about without her jewels. But Puniah saw that her mother and grandmother would not hear of the plan of letting her go with him to Ongole. He went alone. After six months he returned for Subbamah. The mother and grandmother cried, and made a great noise in the village. But people said : "What trouble is there? She goes with her husband." Subbamah said, "I am going." When they were resting under a tree, ten miles out of Ongole, Puniah said to Subbamah—as he pointed to a large bracelet on each arm and several toe-rings, all made of a kind of pewter, "These will not look well in Ongole." She said, "Then take them away." Her bangles she kept. With considerable pride Puniah took her to say salaam to the Dora and Dorasani, and they said, "She is a nice woman."

The years passed, and Puniah became a preacher who showed ability to carry every additional responsibility that was laid upon him. Subbamah had little children about her, but her mother helped her take care of them while she taught in the school which she and Puniah had started. One day a visitor, Kollum Ramiah, came to them, who was in trouble. He believed in Jesus Christ, but most of the members of his family were against him.

Puniah had been in this man's village, and had been invited to his house. Wherever he went in the village, whether he talked to a group of women pounding rice or spoke to the children at play, Ramiah had followed him. In the evening he had killed a fowl and given it to his wife, saying, "Make a good curry for our guest." And he heard, where he sat, how the old mother grumbled and said, "Is this man our relative that you should prepare such good food for him?" That night Ramiah trimmed the wick of the little oil-lamp, poured in a plentiful supply of cocoa-nut oil, and placed it on a post in a sheltered corner, where the wind could not play with the flame. The rest went to sleep, but Puniah and Ramiah sat together till dawn, and talked about this new religion. And Ramiah said: "I believe in Jesus Christ. All I have done thus far to get salvation was useless."

Ramiah's wife was on his side; otherwise he stood alone in his family. But she too was full of trouble. Her husband's mother told her in spiteful words that she was to blame for all the evil which was coming upon them. Why did she not tell her husband that she would leave him if he joined those Christians? But her husband saw the pressure brought to bear upon her. He said to her, in the presence of the whole family: "If you will come with me, I am glad—come. If you do not want to come, then you must stay, but I shall not stay with you. On your account I am not willing to lose the salvation of my soul." With a sense of great relief she said: "Where you go, I shall go too. Why should I stay where you are not?" No one could, after this, put the blame upon her.

When Ramiah saw that his baptism would make him an outcast in his own family, the hope came that perhaps some of his wife's relations would unite with him. He made a journey of sixty miles on foot, and was kindly received by his wife's uncle and brothers. They belonged to the Nasriah sect, and, therefore, looked leniently on the step which Ramiah was about to take. They said, "Come with us to the annual feast at Tiprantakamu; another branch of the family living farther west will meet us there, and together we will hear what you have to tell us."

The journey was undertaken; and under a large banyan tree in Tiprantakamu the family sat down together for a council. Ramiah announced boldly, "There is no other way to salvation but through Christ. Why should we continue to follow false roads?"

The uncle of his wife, by reason of his age and dignity, was the head of the whole family. He replied, "Nasriah told us to follow him like children, and he would lead us on the way to salvation."

Ramiah said: "You do not follow Nasriah either. He said, 'Do not worship idols.' But you still bow to Poleramah and Mahalakshmi."

His wife's eldest brother looked at the matter from a different point of view. He said: "That Christian religion may be the true religion, but we cannot bear it. Nasriah said, 'Do not drink sarai, do not steal, do not commit other sins'; but no one asks us whether we are living by Nasriah's rule. If we become Christians we shall have to walk carefully. It is too hard. How can a man live by the Christian rule?"

There was a murmur of approval from the family circle. It was certainly more convenient to remain in the Nasriah sect. The Christian standard of living seemed too severe.

Ramiah appealed to them to give up their idol worship and come with him. But the discussion was losing its interest for them. There was talking back and forth to no purpose.

Finally, the aunt of Ramiah's wife spoke. She was a shrewd woman, and was accustomed to being heard whenever she had a remark to make, which occurred frequently. She said: "We have good food to eat now, because we bow to Poleramah and Ankalamah. If we stop bowing before them we may have nothing to eat but a little porridge with pepper sauce poured over it."

This was a practical solution of the question which pleased every one. Several rose up and stretched themselves as a sign that they considered the discussion ended. Ramiah said, "Then, for the sake of your food, you are willing to lose your souls." And he too rose to go, for he knew that he had failed.

On his way home Ramiah visited Puniah and talked the matter over with him. Puniah told him of men who, like him, were outcasts for a time, but whose families finally came with them. Ramiah was full of hope when he found, on his arrival at home, that his father and two younger brothers listened to him gladly. But his father was a meek and quiet man, and feared his wife, and his brothers hesitated and looked to him to take the first step. Ramiah felt the time had come to act. He went to Ongole and was baptized.

As he approached his village on his return from Ongole, he found his wife sitting by the wayside, her little boy asleep in her arms. She thought he might be returning about this time, and sat there waiting for him. "What shall we do?" she said; "your mother is full of anger, and says she will not let you come into the house."

"Never mind," was the calm reply; "we shall find a place somewhere." They slowly walked to the house, and found the mother in front of it, pounding rice for the evening meal. When she saw her eldest son, and noticed, as he took off his turban, that the juttu was gone, she said, in a voice choked with fierce emotion,—

"I brought you forth and cared for you, in the hope that in my old age I should be cared for by you. You have gone on a road on which we shall not follow you. Henceforth I shall not eat food that comes from your hands. Go away! You are to me as those who are dead!"

Ramiah had too long been a man of weight in his walks in life to submit to oppression now. With a firm step he walked into the house as one who has his home there. His younger brothers had neglected their few acres of ground during his absence. He started out to work early next morning. No one dared interfere with him. But the rules of caste were stronger than he. When the family ate, he could not eat with them; the food for him and his wife was put on one side. The village people objected to letting him draw water from their well, lest he pollute it, and they all fall sick. He had to dig a little well for himself, where happily he soon struck water. Those days dragged heavily and wearily.

But the mother's harsh rule could not endure. Her younger sons were baptized, and she dared not repeat her curse when they returned home shorn of their juttus. The old father lay sick, and death was approaching. His sons knew that his soul was thirsting for every word they could tell him of the Christ; but he dared not mention the source of his peace and joy for fear that his wife might speak harshly to him. He died with a quiet faith and trust in Jesus of Nazareth. Ramiah and one of his brothers went to Ongole to school, the youngest stayed at home to support his mother. Outwardly unyielding, she was yet glad to have some one at home on whom she could lean.

A few years had passed when it happened that the youngest son journeyed to see his two brothers at Ongole. While there together, word came to them that their mother, after a short illness, had died. The three men looked at each other. Each knew the thought of the other. But Ramiah hid his face in his hands and wept: "She said that I was as one dead to her, and no food would she accept at my hands in her old age. She has died with her sons far distant, alone, as she said she would be."

There was pain in Ramiah's heart whenever he thought of his mother. Tears came to his eyes when he told of her curse.

A BATTLE-GROUND FOR TWO RELIGIONS

Through Much Tribulation

Not Peace, but a Sword

The Persecutor and His End

THROUGH MUCH TRIBULATION

The wife of Yendluri Rutnam noticed that her husband frequently stopped his work for a few minutes, bent his head over his folded hands, and said as to himself: "O God, I am a sinner. Give me wisdom that I may find the way." She bowed with him. He had told her all he had seen of the Christians in a distant village, where he had gone on trade, and she said, "It must be a good religion."

Bangarapu Thatiah came one day to inquire after the spiritual welfare of his near kinsman. For some reason Rutnam closed his heart against him, and put him off by saying: "Perhaps the Christian sect and the Nasriah sect are only the same thing. I shall remain where I am." Rutnam was proud of the fact that he had been a disciple of the Nasriah sect for ten years.

He had been at Tiprantakamu several times at the annual feast, and had faithfully learned the hymns and verses he had been taught, and fully believed that it must be true that there is only one God. Yet he joined others of the village people when they went to worship the swami Gurapudu, who was supposed to have his home in a margosa tree at one end of the village.

The old men of the village said that there once lived a man, Gurapudu, who died suddenly in a very mysterious way. As usual, the relatives took an earthen pot full of cooked rice to the grave, and laid it in two heaps. Each in turn took a handful of the rice from one heap and put it on the other, to go through the form of giving. Then they sat down at a distance to watch. Had the crows come and eaten they would have known that Gurapudu thought kindly of them. The Madigas believe that as the crows fly away the soul of the dead is liberated from the body, and on the fluttering wings of the crows hastens to some good place.

But at the grave of Gurapudu the crows did not come to eat, and thus his relatives knew that his soul was hovering near the earth, and that he would do them harm. Several had seen peculiar forms hover about a margosa tree in the night, and it was thought best to place a stone under it, paint it with saffron, make large red dots on it, and then worship it. No matter what form Gurapudu might assume, if thus honoured and appeased, he could not go forth to injure the village. The fear of Gurapudu had passed from fathers to sons, for whenever calamity of any kind befell the village, it was regarded as the work of the fiend in the margosa tree.

Thatiah had told Rutnam frankly what he thought of the swami Gurapudu. He met with quiet resistance on this point as on every other, but Thatiah would not be baffled. When a preacher came from Ongole, he told him to go to Rutnam's village, and not to pass his kinsman by. He was a man of tact and education, and had known service in one of the older mission stations before he became the right-hand man of the Ongole Missionary in the early days of the movement among the Madigas. The whole village gathered to hear him. Before he had finished, Rutnam knew wherein the difference between the Nasriah sect and Christianity lay. Moreover, the strange preacher had made sarcastic remarks about the swami Gurapudu, and, while all were laughing, had asked permission to go to the margosa tree near by, take the stone, and hurl it away into a ditch, with all its red and yellow markings. The swami had not taken notice, for nothing happened to the preacher.

Later in the day he had a private talk with Rutnam, and asked him some very searching questions: "Are you a sinner, or one who has accumulated merit? Was your worship of swamis good or bad? You have bowed to idols, have been stealing grain when your Sudra master looked the other way, have worked on Sunday, have eaten carrion; and now what do you think of your work?" Rutnam agreed that it was all bad, and that he must turn away from it. The preacher was satisfied that there was conviction here.

Soon after this Rutnam was ordered by the village Karnam to carry a letter to a distant village. He had to drop all other work and go on this errand, nor could he expect to be paid for it. Some generations back the family had received a grant of four acres of land from the Rajah of Venkatagiri, and in turn for this they had to stand ready to do the bidding of the Karnam. It was Yetti-service, a service exacted under provisions that closely resemble the serfdom of the middle ages. Rutnam tied the letter into his headcloth and went his way. Arrived at Petloor, he approached the Government Office, where the Brahmin clerks and officials sat over their task. He dare not go near, for great would be their wrath if even the air they breathed were polluted by the presence of a poor Madiga. But he stood afar, holding high the letter he had brought, and soon a Sudra servant came to take it from him. They signified to him that he might go, and, after resting in the shade of a tree, he took a roundabout way home.

His object was to see his distant kinsman, Pullikuri Lukshmiah, who, he had heard, had lately been baptized, and had much to say about the worthlessness of Rajayogi Gurus. Lukshmiah received him with every mark of friendship. Sticks were soon burning under a pot of water, that he might bathe after his journey. Odours of spicy curry came from the place where the women were cooking the evening meal; and, as they sat under the tamarind tree, in the cool of the evening, the two men talked together about many things. Lukshmiah saw that some one must speak an authoritative word. He asked, "Have you believed in Jesus Christ?" With a firm voice Rutnam replied, "I have." "Have you been baptized?" "No." "Then go to Ongole this very month and be baptized, lest if you die soon you should go to hell."

Their belief in spirits and demons, in fiends and matris, gives to the more thoughtful minds among the Madigas an intense desire to make sure that they are on the way to a blessed existence beyond the grave. The Christian conception of a heaven and a hell was readily absorbed by them. The hope of the one and the fear of the other are a powerful influence in their moral conduct and religious fervour. And thus the injunctions of Lukshmiah brought to an end the wavering of Rutnam, and shaped the destiny of one of the choice workers of the Ongole mission.

There was an element of refinement in the appearance of Rutnam. His features were regular and of a noble outline. Every passing emotion found expression in his eyes; hence the look of anxiety that became habitual in his later years, stamped there by the many hardships of his life. When met by kindness his face could light up with a rare smile. He was a man who in return for kindness could give devotion.

During the first few years of his ministry he often took his wife with him, to help him as he preached in the villages here and there. This became impracticable. As the converts multiplied the vexation of the Sudras grew. Trouble was heaped upon the preacher and his wife, till Rutnam said, "It is not safe for a woman to face these insults." Henceforth he went alone.

A social revolution on a small scale was in progress during those early years. The Madiga population was fast being Christianized, and in consequence there was a breaking away from economic and social relations that had held the Madigas during many centuries. There was novelty in the desire of the Christians to have one day in seven for purposes of rest and worship. To many a Madiga it had been an unknown accomplishment to remember the days of the week. It raised him decidedly in the scale of human beings when he became sufficiently enlightened to know the days as they passed. He found opportunity to cultivate moral fibre when he began to insist that he must have one day in seven reserved for the worship of his God.

To the Sudra landholder it was a cause of constant irritation to be obliged to reckon with this new spirit of independence on the part of the Madiga. He was accustomed to call his serfs to work whenever he required their service. Day and night, seed-time and harvest, they were to be ready to obey his call. He did not look upon their desire for a Sabbath of rest as a legitimate demand. It seemed to the Sudra usurpation of authority pure and simple. The Karnam shared in the vexation of the Sudras, for when he called the Christian Yettis to work on Sunday, or start on long journeys with heavy burdens on their backs, they asked to be allowed to go the next day.

There was tension in all the region round about.

Whenever some village matri, some fiend or demon, was to receive special worship, the question arose as to the course which should be pursued with the rebellious Madigas. It was part of the service which they owed to the village community, on the principle of mutual service, that they should beat the drums when there was a festival to the swamis. The Madigas had to furnish the leather for the drums. Who should beat them but they? To refuse to perform this old-time duty meant loss to them. They received the carcases of the animals which were slaughtered to please the gods in question as remuneration for their special service.

The trouble culminated in the village Ballapudy, one of the villages in Rutnam's charge. The Madigas rebelled against ancient institutions, and in consequence the organization of the village community was used against them. The potter is the village servant, who makes the earthen pots that break so easily, and, therefore, need frequent replacing. The washermen likewise serve the village. They have their group of houses in the village, and when the village tank is dry, their donkeys take the clothes where there is sufficient water. There was interdependence of various kinds. If by the order of the Munsiff and Karnam the mutual helpfulness of the community was withdrawn from the Madigas, their isolation was of a peculiarly trying nature.

The Karnam of Ballapudy was not a man of strong personality. But he knew that he had power to harass, and decided to take the initiative, and show all the region round about how to deal with these recreant Madigas. Forthwith the village washermen were told not to wash for the Christians; the potter was told not to sell pots to them; their cattle were driven from the common grazing-ground; the Sudras combined in a refusal to give them the usual work of sewing sandals and harness; at harvest-time they were not allowed to help, and thus lost the supply of grain which the Sudras had always granted them. They were boycotted and ostracized on every hand. The Karnam called the heathen Madigas from elsewhere to do the work of the village, and the Christians had no alternative but to go to distant villages to find a little work, and earn a scant pittance. This went on for a season. Rutnam suffered with the distress of his people.

A day of reckoning came when the Ongole Missionary pitched his camp in a grove near the village Ballapudy. He rode through the bazaar of the village, Rutnam and others of the Christians with him, made happy and full of courage by his presence. On one side of the road—his arms deferentially folded over his chest—stood the Karnam. Rutnam pointed him out to the Dora: "That is the man"; and the Karnam made many and deep salaams. The Dora, however, seemed not to notice him. Then the Karnam, already full of fear, grew very anxious, and wondered what would happen to him; for he had heard that the Ongole Missionary was strong in protecting these Madigas.

Walking at a little distance from the horse, the Karnam now began to excuse himself. A large crowd had gathered of all castes. There were Mohammedans too. Ever since the tent had arrived, and the lascars, who came with it, had told the people the hour when they expected their Dora the bazaar of the village Ballapudy had been filling with people who had come in from villages near by. Many were interested in the issue. If the Dora failed to influence the Karnam, it would go hard with the Madigas in all that region; for other Karnams stood ready to resort to stringent measures.

But here was the Dora not even looking in the direction of the anxious Karnam; the little group of persecuted men and women gathered closely around him. He did not even seem to hear the Karnam's excuses, till, finally, insisting on being heard, the Karnam said: "I did not do that work. There are no witnesses."

Then the Dora's horse stood still, and it turned in the direction of the trembling Karnam. It was a fine white animal; the preachers in the old days were proud of it. Once in the early days, when the mission was in debt, the Dora offered to sell his horse, that he might give the money to his preachers, but they pleaded for the horse. "Never mind about us," they said, "but keep the horse. What should we say to all who stand ready to persecute us if they asked us whether our Dora no longer rides a horse?"

As Rutnam told me the story of the encounter between the Dora and the Karnam, he remembered specially the Dora's horse. "How would it have looked if our Dora had walked through all that crowd on his feet?" And one word of the Missionary was treasured in Rutnam's heart with peculiar gratitude. The Dora said to the Karnam: "You say there are no witnesses. The Christians have told me what you did. The preacher, who is like my 'Tamurdu,' has told me. Would my younger brother lie to me? You are the liar, not my preacher." Rutnam's face trembled with emotion when he repeated to me, several times over, that before all that crowd of men who were ready to injure and destroy him and his little flock the Dora called him his "Tamurdu."

Like a school-boy the Karnam, in deferential attitude, promised to cease from evil-doing. Not once, but twice he had to promise that he would not persecute the Christians any more, for the Dora was afraid "of his lying words." He and all who stood there heard to their surprise that these Madigas were God's children, and in God's special care. "Their God," the Missionary said, "is not like your swamis, who hear not and see not. When these poor men pray, God is not far off. Beware how you touch them."

Deeply humiliated, the Karnam went to his house. All had seen that he was a coward, who could oppress those in his power, but trembled in the presence of one who could call him to account for his actions. Many a man in that region, whose heart was full of anger against the Christians, decided to let others persecute them if they would, but that he would hold aloof.

Some years had passed, when the priests of the goddess Ankalamah decided that the annual feast at her temple in the village Muktimulla should be held with unusual pomp. There had been cattle-disease of late, and some of the wells were running dry. They said the goddess was probably angry because she had not of recent years been honoured sufficiently, and they hinted, too, that the Madigas and their refusal to beat the drums had fanned the displeasure of the goddess. Now Ankalamah is one of the ten great Saktis, a form of Parvati, consort of Siva. The Karnam of the village Muktimulla was a Brahmin, seventy years of age, and

MADIGAS WITH THEIR DRUMS.

[Page 215.

a worshipper of Siva. He decided that Ankalamah should have the drums beaten by the Madigas at her annual feast, just as she had seen it done during many a century. Moreover, she should have the pleasure of seeing the rebellious Madigas humiliated as they deserved.

When the feast was in course of preparation, and crowds of worshippers had gathered, the Karnam sent for the Christians to come and beat the drums. They returned a message that their religion forbade them to have anything to do with idol-worship. Five village constables were then sent to fetch five of the leading Christians. They were brought by force. Water was poured over their heads until it was thought the uncleanness of their Christian religion had been washed away. Their heads were shaved, and only a lock on top of their heads—the juttu—was left, that the swami might dwell therein. And, finally, their foreheads were marked like those of the other worshippers. The drums were forced into their hands, and for three days they had to endure the shame of their position, while large crowds came to worship the goddess.

Rutnam hastened to the spot. These men were members of his flock. But what could he do? What could be done even if they should unite in resistance? They were overpowered by numbers. The five men had gathered up the hair as it fell under the razor, and had tied it into their cloth. As soon as release came, they hastened to Ongole and told their tale to the Missionary, showing the hair in their cloth, taking off their turbans to show the bald heads that represented to them mutilation.

A case was filed in the criminal court. The English magistrate of Ongole tried the case in person. He asked the five Christians whether they considered themselves to have been insulted. They said, "It was as if our throats had been cut; our shame was so great." Rutnam and two Christian teachers were the witnesses on the one side, a crowd of false witnesses stood on the other side. The legal proceedings took some time, and then judgment was passed. Since the Karnam was an old man, he was spared the three years of imprisonment which he deserved. He had to pay a fine of thirty rupees, and was imprisoned for three months. As he was a Brahmin, imprisonment meant pollution of the very worst kind. He died four days after his release. His son took his place. When I asked Rutnam whether the son was better than the father, he replied, "Can a tiger have young jackals as children?"

Thus the government, which has made itself, in a measure, the vehicle of Christian principles, took no notice of Ankalamah's desire to see the drums forced into the hands of defenceless Madigas. The violation of the law of religious toleration carries with it a maximum punishment of five years' imprisonment. That an aged Brahmin, in respected position, should have been deeply humiliated because he insulted the religious belief of five men, who were of the outcasts, and in former days considered too low to come within the same jurisdiction that applied to the members of other castes, was, indeed, an indication that a new day had dawned for the remnant of an aboriginal tribe that had known nothing but abject servitude for many centuries.

NOT PEACE, BUT A SWORD

There were four brothers in the Nambadi family. Krishniah was the eldest; upon him fell the chief care of the family when his father died. Anandiah, the second, was the pride of the family. He knew more than was ordinarily expected of the Mala priest, and his learning gave distinction to the priestly functions of the brothers. Venkatiah, next to Anandiah in age, was quiet and retiring, and ever ready to do the bidding of Anandiah. The youngest was Chinna Krishniah. In honour of the god Krishna, one of the incarnations of Vishnu worshipped by the family, it was thought well to have two sons by the name of Krishniah. As is customary in such cases, the older brother was called "big Krishniah," the younger "little Krishniah."

Anandiah was the most active, and at the same time most restless member of the family. He was ever on the alert for something new to learn and to investigate. He had early learned to read, and was always ready for new books. He listened to the singers who relate the events of the past in a peculiar mixture of the legendary and historic. If he met any one whose religious views differed from his own he was ready to argue with him. With his enquiring spirit to urge him on, it is not surprising that Anandiah had a religious history, even before he became a Christian.

The Nambadi family were Malas. They were thrifty, and were counted a prominent family in the Mala community. Their ancestors, so far as they knew, had always been priests. The Vishnuite reformer, Ramanuja, who lived in the twelfth century, is said to have founded seven hundred and fifty priesthoods in Southern India, among all castes and classes. It is not impossible that this Mala family derived their hereditary priesthood directly or indirectly from Ramanuja.

Anandiah, not satisfied with the routine of a priest of the Ramanuja sect, joined in addition the Chermanishta sect. The brothers were little pleased with this new phase in Anandiah's career, but he went his way and kept his own counsel. Silence and mystery are the characteristics of this sect. It was a relief to all concerned when Anandiah, probably by sheer force of reaction, turned to the Rajayogi sect, and became a follower of the Yogi Pothuluri Veerabramham.

That he could pass from one sect to another without exciting comment among those whom he and his brothers served as priests gives evidence of the elasticity and extreme toleration of Hinduism, so long as the institution of caste, which is the basis of social organization, is left untouched. After all, to the thoughtful Hindu, Vishnu and Siva and the many lesser gods of the Hindu Pantheon are but manifestations of the one great deity, the Parameswara. This toleration does not extend to the religion of Christ; the upheaval which ensues where it enters is dreaded. It is inimical to caste, and thus revolutionizes social relations. Its pure theism, with the divine incarnation of the God-man, Jesus Christ, raises the mind above the need of an image, and thus produces a radical change, which places a gulf between the Christian and the members of various sects of Hinduism.

As Anandiah went about among the people in his office as priest, he was often asked about the attractively bound booklets which the faithful Pentiah from Ongole was selling everywhere. Though always ready to investigate a new belief, Anandiah in this case had strong misgivings. He took the tracts, looked them over carefully, until he had become fully aware of the contents, and then told the owners that these were bad books, and whether it would not be best to tear them into pieces. Thus he publicly tore up many a tract which Pentiah had sold in that region.

One day Anandiah met Pentiah in the way, and in a somewhat hostile spirit asked him concerning himself and his religion. Now Pentiah was not the man to face Anandiah in argument. But he had faith, and he had conviction; he told Anandiah, with all the force of his simple, devout nature, that idolatry was evil, and that there was no salvation in Hindu sects. He spoke of Jesus Christ as a living reality. His belief in Him as an indwelling presence was the secret of the power which this simple-hearted man wielded over men.

Pentiah was of Mala extraction, and the Mala priest, Anandiah, could, therefore, talk with him about the social aspects of the Christian mission that had lately been established in Ongole. He had heard that a number of Madigas had already joined it; what became of social relations in a mixture of castes? Outcasts equally, the Malas and Madigas hold aloof from each other. They have separate wells; they do not eat together, nor do they inter-marry.

It was not necessary to convince Anandiah that caste was a system which could not be upheld as containing divine truth. He had seen it attacked in the midnight orgies of the Chermanishta sect, and he knew that the Yogi Pothuluri Veerabramham had prophesied a day when caste distinction would cease. He wanted to know what practical solution Christianity had to offer. Pentiah told him that there was no caste in the mission compound at Ongole, that all drank from the same well, nor did they hesitate to eat together. If any one was found to cling to the old distinction between Mala and Madiga, he was rebuked. It was a new life, of which Pentiah thus gave him a glimpse. Anandiah did not commit himself, for his thoughts were seething within him, and Pentiah went his way.

It happened soon after this conversation that the four brothers went to a village at some distance to perform the Bhagvatum. Anandiah entered upon the undertaking in a half-hearted way. Six rupees was the price agreed upon for the night's work, and he was determined to go through with his part. They began after dark in the evening, and continued till dawn. A fine, moonlight night had been chosen. Torches were held where the actors were in full view. The people from neighbouring villages had come, and sat on the ground, in the large open space in front of the village, ready to enjoy themselves during their days of leisure, for the harvest was over and seed-sowing time had not yet come.

The brothers had been joined by relatives who lived some twenty miles away. The performance required ten actors. Anandiah played the chief part; he recited the accompanying passages of the drama as they passed from one act to the next. The Telugu of the text was much intermingled with difficult Sanscrit expressions, and he often stopped to explain the meaning. The main episodes in the life of Krishna were the subject of the play. The mother and wives of Krishna played an important part, and the brothers, therefore, wore the apparel of women and decked themselves with the jewellery of women. It was, in the Hindu sense, a religious play, yet the buffoon was not wanting, and his part of the performance brought the play to a low level.

At last the cocks in the village began to crow, and the birds in the trees stirred with busy chatter; the darkness of night shaded into the grey tints of dawn; the little oil-lamps that had been placed here and there were extinguished, and both actors and spectators lay down for a few hours of sleep. Anandiah went away to one side, sat down under a tree, and busied himself reading the *Gnanabodha*, a book which Pentiah had left in his hands. Several gathered around him, and he read to them, and explained also what he had read.

Noon came, and the feast which concluded the performance of the Bhagvatum was ready. Pedda Krishniah was to perform puja before the idols of Krishna, and then all were to eat. The sleepers rose, and the brothers went to call Anandiah. He said, "I am not coming." "Why will you not come?" His reply sent consternation to the hearts of the brothers: "I have even now believed in Jesus Christ, and will no longer have anything to do with idols, nor will I eat anything where idols have been near the food."

Anandiah had suffered deeply in mind all that night, and the turning-point had now come. The brothers grew angry. He had told them of his intention before the people, and they asked him right there, "Are you going into that Madiga sect?" "Yes." "Are you going to eat with them?" "I shall eat." "Then we shall not let you into the house." "I shall not come if you don't want me."

Anger was out of place in the face of such determination. The brothers hid their dismay as best they could, and directed their attention to the present moment. Anandiah had done the hardest part of the work, and it was now their duty to see that he had to eat. They said, "Before we worship the idols, we will send you of the food; eat it wherever you like; even though you join that sect you shall not go hungry." He suspected that more mantras would be said over his food than over the other. His disgust over night had grown beyond endurance. He replied, "I will have nothing to do with that food."

They wanted to know where he would eat. He pointed to the house of Malas who were friends, and said they would give him to eat. "But," the brothers said, "that is not nice food; we shall send you nice meat curry." This consideration had no power to move Anandiah. "Even though you send nice food, I shall not touch it. I prefer porridge to what you can give me." Baffled in their intention, they muttered, "Very well; eat what you like," and went away and left him.

The brothers felt more like crying than like eating the feast that was first offered to the idols and then placed before them. Heavy losses were before them if Anandiah failed them. The part which he took in the performance of the Bhagvatum required more knowledge than they possessed. After they had eaten, they sat down under a tree and waited the coming of Anandiah. "You have lost a very nice meal," they said as he joined them. "And you have brought punishment upon yourselves by eating yours," was his reply.

But they were anxious to know their fate. When Anandiah belonged to the Chermanishta sect, the brothers knew that midnight orgies of a very doubtful nature took place twice a year; but they knew not what they were, and asked no questions, for Anandiah still played the Bhagvatum. They were willing again to bear with his belief, but the question was: Would he play the Bhagvatum after he had become a Christian? Pedda Krishniah, therefore, asked him: "When you were in the Ramanuja sect you played the Bhagvatum; in the Chermanishta sect you played; you became a Rajayogi, and yet played. Now that you have become a Christian are you going to play?" Anandiah replied, "I shall never again play."

The brothers then turned to the financial aspect

of the question. They had been asked to perform in several villages. Gain, aggregating one hundred rupees, was in sight. Would he remain with them for one month more? He refused to join them even for one day.

They then tried threats. "We shall influence your wife so that she will not hear your word." But threats had no effect on Anandiah; he heeded them not.

Once more they appealed to him: "You are a well-read man; you write poetry; but now are you gone mad. How do you expect to make your living?" Anandiah was weary; he said: "Don't ask me that; God will show me. If He does not see fit to feed me, I'll die."

Argument, threat, and appeal had failed to produce any effect. The brothers were silent. It was the lull that precedes the heavier outburst of the storm. They had been proud of Anandiah, nor could the angry excitement of the occasion wholly hide the brotherly affection that shone from their eyes as they asked him very quietly, "Then you will not remain with us?" He shook his head.

The four brothers rose to go home. Two of them hastened, so as to gain time to influence Anandiah's wife before his arrival. He had married her about six months previously, soon after he had become a Rajayogi. She was fourteen years of age, old enough to meet him with every display of anger when he appeared. In the excited fashion of Hindu women she cried, "I don't want you any more. I shall go back to my parents!" The brothers tried to prevent Anandiah's entrance into the house, but he quietly came in as usual. They told the mother not to give him food, and she agreed that she would not; but secretly she gave him all he wanted.

Anandiah was now an outcast. The brothers told the village people that he had gone mad. As the days passed Pedda Krishniah's heart grew very hard within him. He went to the Malas in other villages and said: "Anandiah has joined that Christian sect, has eaten with the Madigas, and a devil is in him. If he asks you for water, do not give it to him." He never made salaam to Anandiah, and if he saw him coming one road he took the other. The mother remained firm in befriending Anandiah. She was first a mother and then a Hindu. Anandiah was her son, and she insisted upon giving him an abundant share of well-cooked food just as before, no matter how much she might dislike his new belief. Her presence restrained the angry passions of her sons.

Though he had lost his previous employment, Anandiah would not eat the bread of idleness, and, therefore, began to get the daily supply of grass for the cattle that belonged to the family. This was work which had been done by the women of the household. In turn he demanded his food. The brothers knew that in justice he could claim as his own the largest share of their possessions, and that his self-allotted task was unworthy of his position among them. But as they went without him here and there to perform their priestly rites, they realized how much they had depended upon him, and daily their vexation grew, for people asked them about the madness that possessed Anandiah. In time it was noticed that Venkatiah was very friendly with Anandiah; they often talked together, and seemed to be of one mind. The mother, too, was seen to lean toward Anandiah.

Pedda Krishniah and Chinna Krishniah now found that they were on one side, and Anandiah, Venkatiah, and their mother on the other; yet they were the ones who kept the family income to something approaching their former thrift. They grew very bitter, and finally they joined together for a quarrel. Their charge was that Anandiah and Venkatiah were not helping them in their work as Gurus; that the Bhagvatum could no longer be performed by the brothers; that they were preaching this Christian religion all the time, and besides were doing nothing. They wanted to know how they expected to live. They had their grievance; but the other side, too, felt that they had borne to the utmost, and declared that the two Krishniahs had gone too far in thus beginning an open quarrel. They signified their intention of leaving. Venkatiah's wife was already in Morampudy. Anandiah's wife, who continued in angry reserve, was ready to go with them, for her father's house was there.

Thus they withdrew, and the two Krishniahs had the field to themselves.

Anandiah and Venkatiah had now turned away from the old life, and the new lay before them had they chosen to enter upon it. They left their wives in Morampudy and journeyed to Ongole to see the Missionary. They talked with him and with some of his preachers, and profited by the experience of others. The Missionary respected their motives when they finally told him that they could not be baptized now—they must first win over the members of their household, lest their hearts grow still harder. With faith strengthened and courage fresh, they turned their faces homeward, though they knew what their reception would be. Rumour that they had in fact been baptized had preceded them, and the two Krishniahs had been told in several places that they were no longer acceptable as Gurus. Nothing daunted, Anandiah and Venkatiah now proceeded according to a definite plan. They went to the villages round about to preach, and sometimes stayed away for several days. There was no lack of food wherever they went; they were Christian preachers even before their baptism.

The two Krishniahs said, "They are growing more spiritually-minded; let us take away their books." Wherever they could find one they stealthily took it away; but the fountain of spiritual life in their brothers had a source far beyond the books which were now so often missing. It was not long before people began to come to the house to ask Anandiah to read to them. This roused the fierce jealousy of the two Krishniahs. They invariably took the *Ramayana*, or the *Bhagavata-Purana*, and sat near by, calling Anandiah's listeners to come away and hear the wonderful tales of their own gods.

The home of the Nambadi family had now become a battle-ground for two religions. The two Krishniahs knew they were losing ground, yet did their best to hold their own, and they enjoyed all the advantages which conservatism grants. They had the past on their side; their belief and their practices had the sanction of centuries of usage. Anandiah and Venkatiah were innovators, heretics, whose end in view was an upheaval of social relations and the subversion of old-time faith. Their attitude, however, was characterized by meekness. Anandiah, whose word had formerly been respected and feared, was now silent when treated as one whose presence was merely endured. The mother had occasion to tell Chinna Krishniah that Anandiah was his elder brother and knew more than he, and that he should not forget this, even though Anandiah was a Christian.

Months passed, and then it was noticed that the joy of anticipation shone in the faces of Anandiah and Venkatiah. The reason for this joyousness was that the Ongole Missionary was coming, and would camp in the grove near their village. In those days, thirty years ago, it was not necessary to send a messenger here and there to ask people to come and hear what the Missionary had to say. The word spread, and was rapidly passed from village to village. From the time that the tent arrived and was unloaded from the carts and pitched ready for its occupant, Anandiah and Venkatiah were scarcely seen at home. The mother, with Pedda Krishniah's wife, went and listened with an open heart. The two women believed all that the Missionary said about Jesus Christ, but they carefully avoided those who might question them about their belief, and went home and were silent. The mother could not bear to allow anything to rise up as a barrier between herself and her children; Pedda Krishniah's wife was afraid of her husband.

The two Krishniahs said, "Everybody is going; let us go too." They held themselves aloof, and proudly stood on one side, for they realized that it was well known how they had treated their brother Anandiah, and thought that proud indifference was the attitude most becoming under the circumstances. But Anandiah was bent on efforts of a conciliatory nature. At the proper time he called the Missionary's attention to them: "Those are my brothers." The Missionary spoke kindly to them: "Why do you not believe in Jesus Christ?" The brothers showed by their reply that the spirit of Christ had not yet touched their hearts. They asked, "How are we to earn our living?" The Missionary pointed to the birds fluttering here and there in the trees under which the tent had been pitched. He said, "Does not God feed the birds of the air and the fish in the sea?"

They would not have been willing to admit it, but the two Krishniahs went home in a gentler mood and in a kinder frame of mind than they had known for some time. Pedda Krishniah had some thoughts about the Dora. He had never seen one before near by; but he felt certain that if this Dora had stayed in his own country he would not have lacked food and money. This religion could not, therefore, be worthless if this Dora thought enough of it to go about preaching it. None of these thoughts did he mention to Chinna Krishniah.

Anandiah and Venkatiah could not separate themselves from the Missionary and those who were with him. They followed the camp to the next stopping-place, and not a word that the Missionary spoke were they willing to lose. When at last they arrived at home, it was chiefly Chinna Krishniah who, with some of the village people, made light of their zeal. "Why do you come back?" they asked. "Did not your Guru take you straight to heaven?" Pedda Krishniah said nothing. The mother busied herself with the food, but quietly told Chinna Krishniah that his jests at the expense of Anandiah were out of place. He asked, "Are you, too, taken with the same madness?" The village people, wherever Anandiah went, had many questions to ask about the Dora, his horse, his servants, his tents, about his manner of living, and his sayings and doings. Anandiah found that the Dora's short stay among them had given him a degree of prestige in that region, of which he was not slow to take advantage.

Pedda Krishniah, meantime, had had an experience which has always seemed to him a remarkable one. It happened before the Missionary came on tour. He had taken Chinna Krishniah with him to a village at some distance, where a man had died, and the family had requested him to perform the usual ceremonies on the twelfth day after the death, in order to rid the house of all uncleanness. Pedda Krishniah bathed in the prescribed way, and then, in the presence of the whole family, he spread a cloth over a large wooden seat, piled rice upon it, and on the rice he placed the idols sacred to the worship of Vishnu. He conducted puja before the idols. The savoury food which had been prepared from the sheep and several fowls that had been killed, of rice and pappoo, and the various spices that constitute a good curry, accompanied by a pot of the intoxicating sarai, was offered to the idols with the prescribed mantras. There was burning of incense and much feasting and drinking that night until all lay down to sleep.

At sunrise one after another rose, and Pedda Krishniah went to the place where the idols had been left standing on the pile of rice ready for the concluding ceremonies. But, behold, the largest of the idols, nine inches high, made of a mixture of copper, silver, and gold, was gone! It was a Venkateswarurdu idol, and had been handed down, with the other nine idols, from father to son. Pedda Krishniah called the heads of the family and said, "How is this? The largest idol is gone!" They looked everywhere. It was not to be found near the house! They looked farther, and finally found it on a pile of rubbish not far from the house. A dog had come overnight, while all were sleeping soundly after their feasting, had bitten the idol to see whether it was eatable, and had carried it away in its teeth.

Fear fell upon the household. "Perhaps," they said, "the swami is angry, and will not save us from the evil that may fall upon us." They prepared tamarind water, and Pedda Krishniah washed and cleansed the idol in it. He conducted elaborate puja before it; much incense was burned and many mantras were said, and it was hoped that the swami, Venkateswarurdu, would take no offence at the insult that had been offered.

As the two Krishniahs walked home, the bundle of rice which was the priestly due hung over their shoulders, Pedda Krishniah had many thoughts, which, however, he kept to himself. He reasoned in this wise: "If we have a swami to which we make puja, can the dog carry it off in its teeth? We put up a swami to give it food; it can't say, It is not enough. It can't say to the dog, Don't carry me off. How can such a swami save me? This is mere illusion."

Pedda Krishniah was a changed man after this experience. The dog that carried away his Venkateswarurdu idol in its teeth caused his belief in idols to totter. But he gave no outward sign of the fact that his intellect no longer furnished assent to the hardness of his heart and the determination of his will. The conflict was there, and the Missionary's visit only hastened the crisis. He would not yield, however, until he found that he could no longer perform the offices of a priest, even though he would. Of this he soon became convinced.

The two Krishniahs were asked to conduct a household ceremony in a neighbouring village. While on their way they talked together. Pedda Krishniah said: "What do you really think of this Christian religion? Is it good or bad?" His brother said: "Why do you ask me? Say yourself." Pedda Krishniah then expressed his conviction that it must be a true religion. "We are making fun of Anandiah and Venkatiah," he said, "but we are doing wrong. What they are doing is right." It was in a very peculiar frame of mind that he proceeded to conduct the puja. As he took up each idol to put it in its place, he looked toward Chinna Krishniah with a smile of contempt.

The household assembled remonstrated: "We feel weak, for you are not performing the functions of your priesthood with faith!" He then tried to keep up appearances, but his hands shook, he trembled and could hardly proceed. He wondered what would happen, for he had never before thus trembled. He could not say more than part of the usual mantras, and prepared to go home earlier than he was wont. The village people tried to keep him over night, but he refused. Chinna Krishniah was now in great sorrow. He said on their way home: "Brother, it seems you, too, are going to that religion. Then I shall go away to another country." But his brother comforted him: "Don't be afraid. We two will stay together as the other two are doing."

Of the experiences of the night that followed, Pedda Krishniah speaks as follows: "Two men got into my breast, and there was a big fight till morning. Good thoughts came, bad thoughts came. One voice said, 'If you believe in Jesus

Christ, you will be blessed.' Another voice said: 'What will you get? Did not your forefathers get heaven? What do you want of this religion?' Thus I went on the whole night without sleeping. I could not pray; I could only say within myself, 'O God, take away my sins and let me get to Thy heaven.' Towards morning I looked on the beam under the thatch of the roof to see whether Anandiah had left any of his books there. I took and read, and then peace came into my mind."

Pedda Krishniah's struggle was now ended, but where was Anandiah meantime? "Hope deferred maketh the heart sick." Perhaps it was partly the strain of long waiting and patient endurance that caused his physical strength to ebb low. He was sick, and was staying with friends in a village not far away, who had through him believed in Jesus Christ, but, like him, had not yet been baptized. Pedda Krishniah asked the mother on the morning that brought him peace, "Where is Anandiah?" She told him, and there was silent reproach in the tone of her voice which stung him to the quick.

He went out on the road by which Anandiah must come, and ere long saw him in the distance, leaning on his staff. He, who had often avoided the road by which Anandiah was to come, now walked towards him and made a salaam to him. Anandiah stood still. Not for many months had Pedda Krishniah said salaam to him. He looked at him, and, behold, the hard look was gone from his face. He fell upon his neck and asked: "My brother, how has God changed your heart? How has He given you a mind to come on this better way?" They embraced each other, for the brotherly affection, so long pent up, at last asserted itself. During eighteen months Pedda Krishniah had had, as he to-day says, "a hard devil within." By sheer reaction the tears now flowed freely as he told Anandiah his whole experience—of the dog that carried away the Venkateswarurdu idol, of the hands that trembled so that he could not perform puja, of the sleepless night when two men were fighting within him.

Anandiah, too, had an experience to relate. He had joined with the friends with whom he was staying in a prayer that, within ten days,

Pedda Krishniah might yield and become a follower of Jesus Christ. "Oh, my brother," he said, "for eight days have I prayed for you; there were yet two days. Last night I had a dream that you and I were praying together, and this morning I could not stay, I came quickly to see whether the change had been wrought."

They went to the house together. Anandiah said, "Bring your wife, and we will read and pray." She was sweeping when he called her, but so glad was she to come, she dropped her broom and joined them. The mother came, glad and thankful as such mothers only can be whose abounding love keeps families united. Venkatiah came. All in the house came; and then Pedda Krishniah saw how they had borne with him in long-suffering and kindness these many months. He tried to join them as they sang one of the Christian hymns they had learned; he listened as Anandiah read the seventh chapter in Matthew; he could not pray, but he knelt while Anandiah prayed.

The family then had a talk together. Anandiah said: "In a few days Bangarapu Thatiah will pass through here on his way to Ongole to the monthly meeting. Let us go with him and be baptized." Pedda Krishniah was not ready. He said: "You go. I have yet to collect a quantity of grain which is due to me here and there on account of the puja I conducted. I'll gather that in, and after a month I, too, will come." Anandiah would not consent to this plan. He argued with his brother, and finally capped the climax by asking, "If you should die while gathering this grain, where would you go?" So Pedda Krishniah agreed, and left behind him all that was his as a Mala priest and turned from his priesthood.

The family was not yet a united one. Chinna Krishniah was sorely grieved. At night he slept on one side, and by day he held himself aloof. He was planning to leave his brothers and to join other Mala priests. But the brothers talked kindly to him; they told him that they wanted to go to Ongole to be baptized, and asked him to put away all anger and consider the question carefully. His heart was softened, and he became the youngest disciple among them.

Bangarapu Thatiah arrived with his staff in his hand. He would not sit down and rest until he had heard all. With his quiet dignity and simplicity he said : "God has given this. I prayed for it."

The four brothers became Christian preachers. Three of them left home, and were placed at the outposts of the movement of the Madigas toward Christianity. The mother lived to a ripe old age in the old home with Pedda Krishniah. The coming of Christianity had strangely affected the lives of her sons; all would have been different if they had remained Mala priests. But she had no regrets, only joy; because she knew that salvation comes through none other but Jesus Christ.

THE PERSECUTOR AND HIS END

Under the shade of a tree at one end of the village bazaar of Kutchipudy, a number of Sudras were sitting in conversation more animated than usual.

"They will become like Doras, and will refuse to listen to our orders," said one of the Sudras.

"They now have a school as large as ours. After they learn to read, how will they do our work?" said another.

"I had a bullock," said a third, "which was sick several weeks. It died, and I called the Madigas. They took it away outside the village, secured the hide and buried the rest. When I bargained with them for the sandals which they must give in turn, they refused to give as much as formerly. I told them I gave them the whole bullock; why did they bury the meat? 'Such filth,' they said, 'shall not come into our village any more.' What shall we do with them? They are undoing the customs of our fathers."

The Munsiff of the village, Ballavanti Durgiah Naidu, had thus far been silent. Now he took up the turban that lay by his side, put it on, and rose up as if to go. "I will teach them," he said. "Ten more have now gone to Ongole to be baptized. When they return I shall force them all to become as heretofore."

Durgiah Naidu was a man of iron will, of relentless harshness, a man who carried to the bitter end what he had once begun. Several of the Sudras looked at him as he rose. They meant no ill. They and their fathers before them had considered themselves in a sense the protectors as well as the employers of the Madigas.

One said, in a drawling tone of voice: "They are not disrespectful. Even when they send word they cannot come to work on Sunday, they beg, in polite words, to be allowed to do the work the next day."

Another, who had not noticed the hard look in Durgiah Naidu's face, said: "But where will it end? Soon we shall have to look for some one else to do our work."

After a few days the Munsiff, Durgiah Naidu called ten of the chief men in the Madiga hamlet who had become Christians. He said to them: "You have gone to Ongole and have been immersed into the water in the name of Jesus Christ. You are thereby unclean. Unless you here again immerse yourselves in the tank, and wash off that uncleanness, we shall not allow you to enter the village." The tank lay between the Sudra village and the Madiga hamlet, a short distance away from each. The village Karnam had come. The Yettis were there to carry out any orders. Large numbers of Sudras had come to see what would happen, for they knew that Durgiah Naidu intended to take extreme measures. The friends and relatives of the ten Christian men came running from the Madiga hamlet, full of misgivings.

The Christians, though in fear and trembling, refused to do as the Munsiff had ordered. Their preacher stood by and encouraged them; more than this he could not do. The crowd had moved toward the tank, and Durgiah Naidu said, "Go in there and dip yourselves under water, that I may know that the Ongole uncleanness is gone." The men did not move an inch. The Munsiff then ordered the Yettis to put their long sticks on the necks of the Christians and push them under the water. They cried and remonstrated, but the Munsiff shouted: "Dip them under! The uncleanness must go." Most of the men were pushed forward with so much force that they fell into the water. Cruelty was added to the indignities heaped upon them.

This was not enough for the Munsiff. His next step was to force the Christians to resume their former worship. On the bank of the tank there was a stone idol of the goddess Poleramah. With much shouting and confusion a buffalo and a goat were brought and placed before the idol; the Yettis struck the blow, and the warm blood flowed freely over the idol, much to the delight, it was thought, of the goddess, whose thirst for blood is never quenched. The Christians were forced to bow before the idol. Some of the blood was taken from it and their foreheads marked with it.

POLERAMAH AND HER BROTHER.

[*Page*. 250

The horrors of the occasion lasted all night. Specially trained singers had been engaged to relate vile stories about the goddess Poleramah, accompanying themselves by their instruments. Intoxicated with sarai, people danced round the idol. The Christians too were ordered to dance, and again they submitted; their persecutors were in a frenzy of excitement, and resistance would have meant death. A prospective terror was added to the persecutions of the hour when the Munsiff threatened to drag them before the Tahsildar and accuse them of theft. They knew how difficult and almost impossible it would be for them to prove their innocence.

The Sudras now thought that Christianity was literally wiped out of the Madiga hamlet. They reasoned that if one of themselves lost caste in any way, all transgressions could be made null and void if the priest, after performing various ceremonies, burnt the tongue with a golden wire. To apply the proceedings of the caste people to those who were outcasts was out of the question. But the measures which had been taken were certainly very rigid, and thus the subject was dismissed for a time. The Christians were in constant fear, and avoided everything that could bring their religious belief into unnecessary prominence. They had told the Ongole Missionary all about the brutal treatment which they had received. He knew how unequal would be the conflict should they try to show resistance, and, therefore, advised them to keep quiet, pray much, and to trust in God, who would yet help them.

Several months had passed, when the news was spread abroad that the Missionary was coming on tour. It was well known that, wherever he camped, he asked for the village Munsiff and the Karnam. He was always polite to them, and asked them to remain and listen to what he told the crowds who came to the tent about Jesus Christ and the great salvation He had brought to men. And generally the village officials showed him every courtesy in return. But there had been occasions when the Missionary found it necessary to emphasize to village authorities that the welfare of these despised Madigas was of importance to him.

Even before the tent arrived in the grove near Kutchipudy the whole village knew what happened in a neighbouring village, where the Dora had his camp. The Brahmins had come to him *en masse* to demand redress, because some Christians, coming from a distance, had passed through their bazaar on their way to the camp. It was an old time custom for the Madiga to step far off to one side whenever a Brahmin passed, for even the wind that had swept over the Madiga was considered polluting to the Brahmin. The Christians were fast outgrowing this aspect of their former abject condition. When the Brahmins that day had called to them to leave the road, and had stood in their way to prevent their advance, it had happened that a Christian woman, by accident, had touched a Brahmin. Much indignation, therefore, was felt in the little Brahmin community. No satisfaction, however, was to be gained from the call on the Missionary. He told them that the bazaar was a public thoroughfare, and was for all; and that if they did not want to be touched, they must step to one side. This, indeed, meant an upheaval of the social relations of the past! It was equivalent to saying that a Brahmin should step aside to let a Madiga pass!

There was great excitement, therefore, in Kutchipudy when the Missionary arrived. He gave the morning to the Christians, and for the afternoon invited the Munsiff, Durgiah Naidu, to his tent for an interview. Few people remained in their houses that afternoon; hundreds gathered about the tent. The Missionary received Durgiah Naidu politely, offered him a chair in his tent, and talked and remonstrated with him at length. Those who were outside, looking into the wide-open tent doors, were disappointed, for there was no scene. The preacher of Kutchipudy, and others of the preachers who accompanied the Missionary on his tour, sat with him in the tent.

It seems the Missionary tried to show to the Munsiff that he was guilty of a usurpation of power, and that he was doing contrary to the spirit of the English Government. The Dora talked in this wise: "The Queen is our mother, and you are eating her pay. You ought, therefore, to treat all her subjects alike; you have no right under English law to persecute these Christians. Many letters have come to me full of the troubles you have heaped upon them. You are doing wrong, and God sees your doings. As a Christian, and as one who knows that you are doing contrary to the wishes of the rulers of this country, I ask you to stop." It was said among those present that Durgiah Naidu, who was a large, portly man, for he was rich and lived well, went into the tent breathing somewhat excitedly, wondering what the Missionary, who had travelled so far to look after his doings, would say to him. When he saw that he was to be merely admonished, he, in the words of the spectators, "breathed comfortably like a frog." He agreed, finally, that he would cease from persecuting the Christians and would treat them kindly.

Durgiah Naidu had been under the impression that the Missionary would leave that night, that all would be as heretofore, and since he and others thought that he had forced the Kutchipudy Christians back into heathenism, it certainly seemed as if he had thus far proved the stronger in the race. Great was his rage when he heard that in the evening, after he had left the Missionary's tent, thirty had asked for baptism, that the Dora had put them off, telling them that they needed much faith to stand firmly in this place, but that they had insisted that they could bear whatever might come.

In the morning, long before sunrise, the Munsiff took the Yettis and a few of his own servants, and walked past the tank in the direction of the Madiga hamlet. He stood at a distance; the Yettis brought to him the leading men among those who had applied for baptism. In an angry tone he said: "The Dora was going last night. You kept him here. Now go away, or I shall kill you." They saw the look of fierce determination in his face; they trembled before it, and went away across the fields, where his wrath could not reach them.

Durgiah Naidu determined to remain, and, by his presence, to control the situation. He stood on the high bank of the tank, covered with trees, between the Madiga hamlet and the Missionary's tent. Ten of the prominent Sudras, with long sticks in their hands, gathered around him. The sun was just rising when the Missionary came toward the tank. He had heard that some of the Madigas had fled, and had seen how Durgiah

Naidu stood and watched every one who approached his tent.

Now came the encounter which all had expected the previous day. Two men, endowed with strength far above the average, met, one strong in defending the rights of men who, at the hands of Christian teachers, were taking the first step out of a crushing serfdom; the other strong in holding them with the iron grip of conservatism where their ancestors had been held. The Christians gathered around their Dora; his two faithful servants, his lascars and bandy men, too, came. A crowd of Sudras came to see what the issue would be.

Many a time since then has the preacher of Kutchipudy been asked to tell what the Dora said to Durgiah Naidu on that morning. There were many who could prompt him should he forget. These are the words of the Missionary as they to-day live in the memory of the people: "If you thought that I was sleeping last night you were mistaken. After I had slept a few minutes, I jumped in my sleep, and woke up thinking about you. I talked with you yesterday kindly; you this morning violate your promise. Don't you know that the English Government punishes such evil deeds as yours? You are like the frog that wanted to be as large as the ox, and breathed so full of air that it burst. You may yet lose your position."

With a careless insolence the Munsiff said, "If I lose it, what is that to me?"

Then the Dora's wrath knew no bounds. His eyes flashed with fire. "But you will care when you find yourself in prison, and, as a convict, work on the roads, carrying baskets of gravel on your head. Even if the English Government do not make you as if you had never been, God will wipe you out unless you cease from evil-doing. As the hawk darts upon the chicks, so you destroy these Christians. I am a Padre, and have only one tongue, not a double tongue like the snakes, and I tell you the truth, that God is not dead, and that He will reckon with you before many months unless you now stop."

Fear entered the hearts of the Sudras. They moved away from Durgiah Naidu and said: "What use is it to worry these Christians? Why don't you let them alone?" They followed at a distance when the Missionary went to the well in the Madiga village, into which, he had heard, the Munsiff had ordered thuma trees to be thrown—trees that have so strong an odour that they make water almost undrinkable. He requested Durgiah Naidu to let his Yettis remove them, and stood by until the logs of ill-smelling wood had been taken out and thrown at a distance. Then he went to the tank, to the idol Poleramah, and had the whole story of that disgraceful scene repeated to him. He was very sad. He told the Christians to endure for a season, and let all that region witness the faith that was in them. In due time, he assured them, God would either make Durgiah Naidu a changed man, or that He would in some way overrule events, so that deliverance and freedom would be theirs. That day he stayed; but toward evening he mounted his horse and rode to his next camp at Kodalur. His tent followed, and next day the grove where the Missionary had camped was deserted.

The Madigas are not without courage. They will dare and do, showing that long generations past valiant blood flowed in their veins. Those candidates for baptism who had fled before Durgiah Naidu one day determined the next to walk the fifteen miles to Kodalur and receive the ordinance there. There were eighteen of them. When the Missionary saw them he hesitated; but he could not refuse them, for they said they were prepared to stand firmly whatever might befall them.

Durgiah Naidu had seen it clearly demonstrated that the Christian religion cannot be washed off with tank water, and that the worship of Poleramah cannot be forced upon unwilling men with the reeking blood of buffaloes and goats. He did not try this experiment again. Instead, he determined that, since the Christians had loosened the old relation that existed between Sudra and Madiga, they should be shown that under the new *régime* the Sudras had no use for them. In consequence they were shut off from contact with the Sudra part of the village. If they tried to walk the usual roads there were Yettis there to prevent them; if they tried to enter the bazaar of the village they were ordered away; some who resisted were cruelly beaten. No one employed them; they had nothing to eat.

Some of the Sudras remonstrated with Durgiah Naidu, but he declared with an oath, "Though it cost me a cartload of rupees I shall not rest until there is not a Christian left in Kutchipudy."

After an absence of just two months the Missionary reached his home at Ongole. He had made one of the long tours that characterized those early times. Territory now occupied by ten mission stations he in those days regarded as his field. He had visited ninety-eight villages where there were Christians. In twenty-seven different places he had pitched his camp. He had baptized 1,067 believers. The item of interest most discussed by the hundreds who came and went in the mission compound, he found, was the latest development of the Kutchipudy persecution.

At the monthly meeting held soon after there was a general expression of desire to hear particulars of the persecution. On Sunday morning the chapel was crowded with its audience of nearly one thousand people. Before them all the preacher and ten of the leading Christians of Kutchipudy stood to tell their story. It was told with tears, for their hearts were very heavy. It seemed as if they could not endure more. Their children were crying for want of food, and many among them had begun to eat leaves, and were dreading the starvation that stared them in the face.

Several of the older preachers, who knew by experience that the hand of God moves with mighty power, and that the prayer of faith does not pass unheeded, prayed with an earnestness that seemed to look for something unforeseen. All felt that they had a part in this, for if the Munsiff of Kutchipudy could thus drive a village of Christians to the verge of starvation, would not the Sudras everywhere harden their hearts against the Christians, and plunge them into similar distress? The collection was taken; twenty-seven rupees was the amount sent to the sufferers, one rupee for each family. But what could they do with money when the bazaars were closed to them?

The preachers of that region asked that some one be appointed to come to the villages where there were Christians and collect contributions of grain. The choice fell upon one of their number, who soon arrived at Kutchipudy with two cartloads of grain which had been given him, a measure here and a measure there. A new principle was this, the application of which was displayed before the wondering eyes of thousands. The despised Madigas were standing by each other in brotherly love!

It was on the 30th of April that the Yettis of Kutchipudy raised the funeral-pyre for the Munsiff, Ballavanti Durgiah Naidu, applied the torch, and stood at a distance while the fire consumed his mortal remains. The persecutor was dead. A letter was sent to Ongole. The Missionary felt as if in the presence of Almighty God, for had he not told Durgiah Naidu that if he did not cease God would cut him off? The message was passed from village to village. Wherever Yettis went with loads to deliver they told of the death of Durgiah Naidu.

Many now recalled the interview between the Missionary and Durgiah Naidu at sunrise, January 30th. Did he not say, "Within three months God will kill you unless you cease from persecuting these Christians?' On the very day, three months later, he died. Others said they saw the Missionary in his fierce wrath lay his hand on Durgiah Naidu's shoulder, as he warned him of the judgment of the Almighty. In that very place, it was said, the carbuncle or cancer, which defied the skill of native physicians, had appeared, had caused excruciating pain, silently borne, for none should know that the power that had vowed destruction to the Christians was being laid low. And thus death had brought the end. Fear fell upon all; and those who had hatred in their hearts found that their hands trembled when they strove to do harm to the Christians. But thousands who bore the name of Christ, though hushed in awe, took courage, for they saw that their God is not one who hath ears and hears not, eyes, yet seeth not, but that He is a God who fights for those who trust in Him.

There was peace now in the Madiga hamlet of Kutchipudy. The Sudras had drawn away from Durgiah Naidu toward the end, and had said: "You deserve it all. Why did you raise your hand against the Christians?" They now called the Christians to work, and treated them with consideration. But gloom settled over the house of Durgiah Naidu. It was commonly said that the curse of the Missionary rested upon it. The widow went to Kottapakonda to worship Kottapaswami, in the hope that the curse would be removed from her household. She came home and fell sick with cholera. She insisted that the preacher should be called to give her medicine, hoping that thus the power of the curse might be lessened. She died. The two sons grew up, and became heads of families. But there were deaths in the family, and deaths among the cattle, and people said, "It is the curse of the Padre Dora."

Fifteen years had passed, when one day the Missionary again camped in the grove opposite the Christian hamlet, in sight of the tank. The sons of Durgiah Naidu feared to go near. They remembered their father's guilt and his end. The preacher told them not to fear, for were they not kind to the Christians? But they said, "We, too, may die."

Their dead mother's elder brother said: "Shall this go on year after year? The Missionary must remove the curse." He went to one of the preachers, who had come with the camp, and asked him to request the Padre to come to the house of Durgiah Naidu and pray there, for then the curse would no longer hover over the family. The preacher went into the tent with his message. The Missionary asked, "Are they now kind to the Christians?" The preacher assured him that they were. "Give order to have my horse saddled."

The uncle of Durgiah Naidu's sons hastened home and gathered the whole family into the house. They placed a chair for the Missionary, and on the table they put a large plate of sugar and fruit to offer to him. He came with two of his preachers. They were led into the house by the men of the family with every mark of courtesy and respect. The women stood on one side holding their children.

He asked, "Is evil-doing gone out from here?" They said, "All is gone." "Then why do you not believe in the true God?" Several answered him that they would believe.

But now the uncle, who was in one sense head of the family, spoke. "We desire," he said, using very courteous language, "to enjoy the blessing of your God upon our household. Your God hears your prayer, and we believe that if you, here in this spot, ask Him to look upon us with favour that we shall once more be a happy family."

This family group knew nothing of Old Testament dispensation, yet trembled before that law of Jehovah that visits the sins of fathers upon their children. The Missionary and his two preachers, who had come to ask for blessings where he, who had died in iniquity, had cursed the believers of Jehovah, represented the New Testament with its injunctions to "bless them that persecute you." The Missionary asked for peace upon this household. The gloom that had hung over it like a threatening cloud was dispelled. He motioned to his preachers to accept the gift of sugar and fruit, and amid the grateful salaams of all mounted his horse and rode back to his camp.

The idol of Poleramah no longer stands on the bank of the tank at Kutchipudy. It was packed upon one of the Missionary's carts, among the tents, rolled up in huge bundles, and was taken to Ongole, where it stands in the mission compound as a relic of the past.

THE POWER OF CHRISTIANITY

A Great Calamity

A Modern Pentecost

Conclusion

A GREAT CALAMITY

There were many who anxiously watched the clouds in the year 1876, for if another monsoon season passed by with cloudless sky a famine was inevitable.

Various ways and means were used of predicting the evil days that seemed to be near, but the old gardener in the mission compound had a way all his own, and he confidently asserted to every one that without doubt a famine was coming.

"Every day," he said, "the Dora came out on the verandah and looked at a little board with a thin glass bottle on it, and in the bottle there was a little mud. And he looked carefully and said, 'Gardener, there is going to be a famine,' and I said surely it would come."

I did not grasp his meaning. "What sort of board and glass bottle and mud was it?" I asked.

"Is there not one on the verandah now?" and he pointed to the barometer; and then I saw that the old man had taken advantage of the methods of Western science in predicting what was to come.

I knew many who lived through the famine of 1876–78. Those who were children during those years were many of them stunted in growth, and some had a look of premature age on their faces. But old men and women remembered a famine which must have had unusual horrors, for all said, "Men ate men in that famine." I was not willing to believe them, for I had heard my husband say that though thousands died in 1876–78, and men were fierce with the pangs of hunger, he had never seen a trace of cannibalism. When, therefore, some one told me of the famine of 1836, that "men ate men," I always asked whether they knew of any one who had seen it. A woman did tell me that her mother was told by a neighbour that she saw a woman put her child into a pot to boil it. Her voice sank to a whisper as she told me. It seemed too horrible to tell.

A large proportion of the Madigas live so close to the starvation point all the year round that the first failure of crops brought hunger to their door. When another rainy season passed without bringing sufficient moisture to help the seed to sprout, there was great distress. The Madigas went to the Sudras for aid, but they had no harvest to share with them. They themselves had not enough to eat, and were beginning to sell the substantial silver belts and gold bracelets of the family to buy food. But cattle were dying of hunger and thirst, and the Madigas found an occasional meal by picking the morsel of meat off the bones of starved animals. The red fruit of the cactus became desirable food. Many began to eat leaves, seeds and weeds.

The Ongole Missionary's daily visits to the "board, thin bottle and mud inside," showed the anxiety which he felt. He was thinking of ways to meet the approaching calamity. Ten years had passed since he came to Ongole. He counted as his flock 3,269 Christians, nearly all from the

Madigas. He had been among them so much, he knew that they were destitute and poor even when harvests were plentiful. The emaciated figures of men and women that were haunting the compound in ever-increasing numbers, calling to him whenever he appeared in the verandah, "We are dying! we are dying!" showed him that something must be done.

The preachers came and went with careworn aces. They knew something of the activity in the mission bungalow, of appeals for help sent to America, of correspondence with the Government in Madras. Ere long they were sent out with a message that all could earn cooley and enough to eat if they came to Razupallem, where the Missionary had taken a contract for digging. The English Government were undertaking relief work of various kinds. The Buckingham Canal, extending from Madras north to Bezwada, on the East Coast, offered relief work on a large scale. The Ongole Missionary had taken a contract to dig three miles of this canal. The relief camp was to be at Razupallem, ten miles east of Ongole and near the coast.

FAMINE-STRICKEN CHRISTIANS.

[Page 274.

One of the preachers, with twenty coolies to help him, was sent ahead to prepare the camp. The Missionary came and showed him where to put up the rows of huts, forming little streets. There were palm trees and bamboos growing all along the sea-shore. A man was sent out to negotiate with the villagers for palm leaves and bamboo sticks, with which to build the little huts. Several wells had to be dug, not deep, for water was near the surface. The potters in the surrounding villages were given an advance for pots, that the starving crowd might buy for a copper, and boil their meal over a fire of the dry leaves and sticks to be picked up everywhere.

At the appointed time the preachers came into Ongole from far and near with a multitude of starving people. The Missionary had sent Komatis ahead to Razupallem with bags of grain to sell. He sent word to the preacher who was there to be ready, for a great crowd would come in the afternoon. At two o'clock they began to arrive, and as the preacher and his helpers looked over the plain towards Ongole, the advancing multitude seemed to them like a huge ocean-wave rolling upon them. The huts were soon filled. Families had the first consideration. Those who found no room had to lie under the trees.

But the tumult and the contentions of that night! The Missionary, after seeing that each had sufficient in his hands for an evening meal, had come to the camp. He tried to establish order; but who can reason with hungry men? There was bargaining for pots; there was wrangling over the grain. So eager for food were they that three preachers had to walk up and down among the huts to see that the palm leaves and the bamboo sticks were not used for fuel, or that by carelessness the huts were not set on fire as the food was boiling in the pots.

In the morning the digging began. Thirty preachers were made overseers. Crude picks and shovels were supplied. The men did the digging; the women filled baskets with earth, and carried them away on their heads to empty on one side and return.

During those first few days the Missionary insisted that the preachers, too, must dig. "After you come and show me your hands full of blisters,

I shall be certain that you know how it feels to dig, and you will not be hard on any one." He feared that some might assume a harsh attitude when urging the starving people to work. Several preachers told me they shovelled dirt till the blisters rose, and they showed them to the Dora, and he said, "Right; you will make a good overseer."

There were Komati Chetties in Ongole, who thought they would take advantage of the thousands in the camp at Razupallem. They brought grain into the camp that was only half ripe. It was cheap, and people bought it. Sickness increased, and the Missionary, as he went about giving medicine, enquired about the food. "Show me the next Komati who brings spoiled grain into this camp." Soon the preachers sent word to his tent that two Komatis were coming with a new supply. As soon as they saw the Dora coming toward them, they dropped their bags in fear and ran away. The bags were opened, and the half-ripe grain fell into the sand. The Dora stamped upon it with his feet till it was all mixed with sand, and no one could find it to eat it.

After this no grain was sold in the little bazaar of the camp that had not been inspected and pronounced fit to eat.

Wages were good. Those who had worked for a time went home and sent friends and relatives. The sick were brought on litters. Those who were too weak to work were given a subsistence allowance. But there was danger lurking even in the abundance at the camp. Some who came were too hungry to wait; they ate the half-boiled grain out of the pot. And then they lay down and died. Many a time the preachers tried to keep these half-starved arrivals from eating. They gave them "congee" to drink—a kind of gruel—but they would not listen. "Never mind, let me eat; I am dying with hunger"; and the remonstrances of the preachers only angered them in their craving for a substantial meal. There were others so emaciated, no matter how much they ate, they were always hungry. They ate oftener and more than their starved bodies could endure. Soon they were found lying somewhere very still, and those who looked at them found that they were dead.

The death-rate was large. No one knew how many died each day. The living were so full of trouble they could not dig graves for the dead; all they could do was to carry them outside the camp into the cactus hedge. The jackals, dogs, and birds did the rest. There were those whose relations died. None could be found who would dig a deep grave into the hard soil. Yet love clung even where the dullness of despair had taken away the sharp edge of pain. They dug a few feet deep into the sand, and covered the dead one well. At night the howl of the jackals, so like the horrible laughter of fiends and demons, was heard in the distance, and in the morning none cared to go near.

Every one in the camp was sad at heart, and many were full of fear. Cholera was abroad in the camp, and death stared every one in the face. One of the preachers told me how his wife died of cholera on the way to the camp. There were women there without husband or brother to care for them; there were children who had survived their parents, and were now to learn that Christianity is tender toward the fatherless. The roadsides everywhere were lined with the bleaching bones of those who had to lie down on the road to die. The heat was intense, and there was no shade where they were digging. "Our hearts were very heavy," the preachers told me "and our Dora's hair turned white during that year."

Each preacher had about one hundred people working under him. He was responsible for the amount of work which they did, and they received their pay from him every evening. He became acquainted with the company working under him, even though there was much coming and going. Often during the day some of the diggers would sit down for a short rest, and then the preacher would join them and hear them tell, in broken words and a look of utter misery in their eyes, of the scattered families and those who had died; and there was always the wail, "We are all dying!" Then was the time to say comforting words. The people said afterwards, "They told us words which we could not forget."

Distress was so great, no one thought of those demons that have their eyes ever directed to this earth, thirsting for blood. The demons seemed to have joined together to slay the living, and who could stop, in the search for a morsel to eat, to propitiate them all? The terrors of the famine were greater than the terrors inspired by demons. As for comfort and trust and hope, where in all their cults had the Madigas anything to inspire the firm belief that there is a hand that guides all events and guides them in mercy?

As the preachers sat with an occasional group of those who wanted rest, they said, "Our God does not send trouble because He is thirsting for the lives of men. He has let this come upon us because He saw that men were going all wrong—that they were doing puja to gods in whom there is no salvation. Jesus Christ, by dying for us, has taken all our troubles upon Himself." And then the preachers would take their New Testament, which they ever had with them, and they would read verses to the people that seemed like balm on their sore hearts and troubled minds—especially "Come unto Me, all ye that labour and are heavy laden, and I will give you rest." And they went back to work. But after a time they said, "Read us that verse again out of your holy book." Never in any of their cults, not in the Ramanuja sect, nor in the Nasriah sect, had they heard such words! And as they were digging the memory of their old cults grew faint in their minds. In their misery they turned to Jesus Christ for His touch of healing.

The contract for three miles of digging was finished after eight months of work. Rain came. The seed was sown with many mantras, but it rotted in the ground. The crowds that came to the mission bungalow in Ongole were so great that though the Dora stood on the east verandah and gave relief to the men to carry home to their families, and the Dorasani stood on the west verandah daily giving grain to the women who had come with their starving children, it was not enough. Four Christians had to act as policemen, wearing a uniform, the pressure was so great. When the servants carried the noon meal the few yards from the cook-house to the bungalow, they had to hold the dishes high above their heads and start on a run, for there were starved creatures everywhere ready to snatch it from them. Every morning the dead were found in the hedge around the compound. They had come for help, but now had no need of it.

The preachers came in from the field, reporting great distress. The Christians were dying, especially the aged and the children. The Missionary could not journey here and there bringing relief. His presence was imperative at headquarters. He had to make his preachers his stewards. They went about, all over the country, with money to give to the Christians. But they had orders not to refuse any one they met in the way starving who asked for enough to buy a meal. They found men greedy and grasping in their demand for help. Even the finer feelings of family relationship were blunt, as the stronger members of families wrangled with the aged and weak, and begrudged them the help they had received.

Again rain came. Bullocks and buffaloes had died; men harnessed themselves to the ploughs. A crop was growing, but a plague of locusts came and destroyed it. Ships came into the harbour at Madras laden with grain, for Government did its utmost to save the people. For the third time, with the help of the Mansion House Fund, seed-corn was given out plentifully in Ongole to all who asked. Sudras came, and for ten rupees carried away bags of seed-corn worth thirty rupees. They promised to give plentifully to the Madigas of the coming harvest. Many a Sudra had gone to Ongole during the famine to tell the Missionary of his distress, and had come away helped and comforted. And many remembered this in the years that followed. The activity at Ongole, the ceaseless readiness to save from starvation the lowest stratum of society, even the Madigas, was a display of the power of Christianity that was a wonder in the eyes of thousands. "It is a good religion," they said, one and all.

A crop of millet, maturing quickly, tided the people over several months, and then a substantial crop of rice was harvested. A great calamity was over. What were the effects?

A MODERN PENTECOST

As the preachers went about on their fields toward the close of the famine, they saw that hundreds were ready for baptism. In villages where heretofore they had been received in a half-hearted kind of way they now found an open door. People to whom they had talked many a time about Jesus Christ in the years before the famine now told them that they believed in Him.

Those early Ongole preachers were a remarkable group of men. There were several among them who stood head and shoulders above their fellows, born leaders of men. Others, more retiring, were spiritually-minded to an eminent degree. People said of them, "They have faith; when they pray to their God He hears them." Several had the gift of the evangelist; they went where others had not been, and left behind them, as they journeyed, many a village where it was said, "It would be well to join this new religion." The majority of the preachers settled as pastors, making some central village their headquarters, and directing their efforts to all the region round about.

Some of his best men the Missionary placed at the outposts, where they had to hold their own far away from the mission station. Many a man developed ability under the stress of circumstances. The wave of enthusiasm that carried with it the strong did not leave behind the weak; they too pressed forward with a strength not their own. The *esprit-de-corps* of those years must have been of unusual intensity.

Four years before the famine began, a Theological Seminary was opened in Ramapatam. Of the early workers a number were together at school in Ongole for a year. They studied, but they knew that the days were precious. Messages came from far and near, sent by those who had heard only enough to make them eager to hear more. The day came when the Missionary told them that they must go; there were too many calls. He promised them another opportunity for study, but it never came. They went forth, and carried such burdens that never again could they lay them aside even for a season.

Their preaching was characterized neither by profound thinking nor by brilliant oratory. It was just the story of Christ and Him crucified told over and over again. Much as, in the days of primitive Christianity, simple but earnest men told the sublime story of the life and death of Christ to every one, so these men went about making Christ the centre of their thoughts and words. A spirit of tender allegiance to Christ was abroad among the early Ongole Christians that is seldom found among men. They could sit together and weep like children as they repeated to each other the story of the suffering of the Christ. "Such was our love for Him in those days," they said to me.

And now these men came to the Missionary to talk with him about the hundreds, even thousands, who were ready for baptism. But he always said, "Wait till the famine is over." Word had gone out some time ago that no more famine-money would be issued in Ongole; still he feared that the hope of further help might form a motive in the minds of some. During fifteen months there had not been a single baptism. But he knew his field; he had refused large companies who came and asked for baptism. He knew that when once the flood-gates were opened none would be able to stay the tide. A letter came from the Mission Secretary in Boston: "What is this that I hear of your refusing to baptize those who sincerely ask for the ordinance? Who has given you a right to do this?"

In June, 1878, the Missionary wrote to his assistants to come to Vellumpilly, ten miles north of Ongole, where there was a travellers' rest-house by the side of the Gundlacumma River, and a grove of tamarind trees, that they might re-organize their work. As cholera and small-pox were still prevalent in the villages, the danger of bringing these diseases to Ongole was thus avoided. He asked them to bring with them only those Christians who had urgent matters to lay before him and to leave the converts behind. Contrary to orders, the converts followed the preachers, and when the Missionary came to Vellumpilly he was met by a multitude who asked for baptism.

He mounted a wall, where he could look into their faces, and told them he had no further help to give them, and they must return home. They cried: "We do not want help. By the blisters on our hands we can prove to you that we have worked and will continue to work. If the next crop fail we shall die. We want to die as Christians. Baptize us therefore!" He hesitated —again the same cry. Then he withdrew and talked with the preachers, who, as the spokesmen of the people, repeated their request. He dared not refuse longer those who begged to be received into the Church of Christ.

On the first day all gathered under a large banyan-tree, sitting close together on the sand. Many voices tried to join in the hymns that had become general favourites. The volume of sound was discordant, but it gave evidence that men were very much in earnest. And then the Missionary preached on those words that all had learned during the famine—"Come unto Me, all ye that labour." For an hour and a half he talked, and none grew weary; he had borne their trouble with them, and now he could talk out of the fulness of an experience in which all had a part. This sermon struck the key-note of those days by the side of the Gundlacumma River.

Early next morning an enquiry meeting on a large scale began. The Missionary told the preachers to separate the people, each one taking those who belonged to his special field under one of the trees. There were many groups thus scattered; some counted hundreds, some only a few. Over each was the preacher, and to assist him he had the Madiga headmen of the villages represented, and the heads of households. The tribal character of the movement made itself felt, for each group was again subdivided into villages, and then into families. But this gregarious character of a tribal movement had its influence only to a certain extent. There was not a man or woman who was not called upon to give evidence that they had entered upon a new life. The individual had to stand for himself, and each one was made to feel that such was the case.

I asked the old preachers many questions about those days at Vellumpilly. One of them told me: "I was on one side with about one hundred people. The Dora came to me and said: 'Do you know all these people?' I said: 'I do not know them all.' He looked them over with me; he had been in their villages. He told me to send away all those whom I did not know, but they would not go, they stayed around the camp. But I wrote down the names of those only whom I knew." This was evidently the general mode of proceeding.

They told me the story of one of the assistant preachers, who to this day likes to magnify his office, and showed the same characteristic then. He had brought a crowd of people with him, five hundred at least. The Missionary saw them, and called for the preacher who was responsible for that part of the field. "For how many of these people can you bear witness that they are really Christians?" He selected about ten; for the rest he hesitated to take any responsibility.

It was an evil day for the assistant preacher. Some plain words were said to him by the Dora and he and all his company were sent home.

One of my oft-repeated questions was: "How could you tell that a man or woman was a Christian?" They said: "We had many ways of telling. When men and women prayed and sang hymns, we knew that Divine life was in them. But we knew, too, when they stopped drinking sarai, and fighting, and eating carrion, and working on Sundays, there was a change in them, and we could tell." Most of those who were baptized at Vellumpilly were really believers before the famine, but for some reason they had held back. The preachers could tell by the attitude of responsiveness that a change had been wrought. They seem to have felt more care and anxiety about those who were refused the ordinance than those who received it. Hundreds must have been sent away. Even to the present time there are villages where the preachers are greeted with words like these: "We came to Vellumpilly to have our 'juttus' cut off, and to be baptized, but you refused. Now go away to those whom you then accepted. We do not want you."

On the first day, July 2nd, 1878, a beginning was made—614 were baptized; on the next day 2,222 followed; on the third day there were 700 more,—making 3,536 in three days. The multitude gathered on the bank of the Gundlacumma River, where the water at this season of the year is fairly deep. The six ordained preachers took turns, two officiating at a time. The names of the candidates were read. Without delay and without confusion one followed the other. As one preacher pronounced the formula: "I baptize thee in the name of the Father, the Son, and the Holy Ghost," the other preacher had a candidate before him, ready again to speak those words, sacred in the history of the Church, and to baptize him likewise. And thus it was possible to immerse 2,222 in one day.

The Missionary stood by, helping and directing; he did not baptize any one during those days. He represented the link between this event on the bank of an Indian river and the sentiment of the Christian world. There would be joy and gratitude in many hearts at home, he knew. But critics, too, would not be far away, who would charge him with undue haste in admitting into the Church of Christ a multitude who could not have been taught more than the most elementary outline of Christian teaching. Years of excessive toil were at hand, to be spent in the Christian training of this multitude. More were coming. Before the year was over 9,606 members had been added to the Church at Ongole, making a total membership of 13,000. And the years that followed were but a continuation of that year. Once again, in 1890, there was a similar event, when 1,671 were baptized in one day.

But what relation did the famine have to this mass-movement? The distress of those two years—the pangs of starvation and the ravages of pestilence—undoubtedly made many a soul turn to that great and merciful God, of whom the Missionary and his assistants preached not only in words but in deeds. God, in His mighty power, can make even a calamity like famine serve as a means to bring about His own Divine ends. But while the famine was one of the conditions which favoured a mass-movement toward Christianity among the Madigas, it was not a normal, healthful condition.

It seems to me that a far more prominent place has been given to the famine, as a condition favourable to this movement, than it deserves. It is true, first came the famine, with its relief-camp at the canal, and then came the baptism of thousands. There is here a temporal succession, which seems to indicate the relation of cause and effect. But I believe the movement toward Christianity would have taken place in the same proportion if there had not been a famine. The Pentecostal day on the bank of the Gundlacumma River would not have been but for the famine; but those same converts would in all probability have come, in smaller companies at a time, but as the outcome of a steady, normal growth.

The famine ushered in suddenly the second period in the history of the Ongole mission. Abruptness is inimical to the principle of growth in the moral and spiritual, as well as the natural world. During the ten years preceding the famine, the preachers did their pioneer work under favourable circumstances, and the Missionary could widen his borders and strengthen his work throughout. There was normal growth, and the converts came as fast as the mission could care for them. The famine and that which followed was an overwhelming experience. After the veteran preachers had told me much of the years before the famine, and I asked: "Now tell me about the years after the famine," they asked in turn: "What is there to tell? Did not thousands come?" The events were of such huge proportion they could not single out incidents and remember detail.

Starvation implies an experience that is not an elevating process to members of even a strong and noble race. The degraded Madiga was rendered more degraded by the greed with which he sought for a morsel of food. If he had had any possessions, a buffalo, a goat, he had lost them. Emaciated, sick, poor beyond expression, he had to try to regain his footing when the famine was over. Any element of sturdy manhood in him had suffered a shock; he was ready to lean upon any one for support. In this condition the mission took him and sought to make a man of him. It is safe to say that some of the most difficult problems which have confronted the mission since that time were born of the famine.

As men of the early days of the mission told me their individual experience, I could mark the steps essential in leading to conversion; steps conscious to the Western mind, conscious also to these Madiga men and women. In their own way they had come to a conviction of sin—there was repentance, and there were faith and justification. When the mass-movement began, these steps were taken unconsciously; the individual was carried along to some extent by the multitude. The Madiga community was shaken to the foundation; individual experience was merged in the whole. But pervading all there was the element of that deep spiritual life of the ten years preceding the famine. It was as the leaven that leavened the whole lump.

But the Madigas forsook their Gurus of the Rajayogi sect. They brought to the Missionary the idols that were theirs in the Ramanuja sect. Whole bandy-loads of stone images of the serpent, of the phallus of the Siva cult, were carted into the compound at Ongole. The family of the Matangi consulted with those who had contributed toward the expense of her initiation, and with their permission the Christian preacher broke the stick of the Matangi into pieces and tore the basket into shreds. Pots, decorated with shells, sacred to Ellama, were smashed by the hundred. It was a religious upheaval that swept away the old cults of the Madigas with a powerful hand, and there was nothing left in their stead but Jesus alone.

Every degree of spiritual life and energy was represented in the years that followed. There were high courage, persecutions unflinchingly borne, and noble example set. But there was also spiritual apathy, mental and moral stagnation Bangarapu Thatiah brought a woman to me, leading a little boy by the hand, five years after the famine. "This woman," he said, "has been an honour to me and to my Master, Jesus Christ, all over my field. When she became a Christian, her husband said but little. Soon her eldest son died, a bright lad of sixteen. Her husband began to ill-treat her, and to say the boy had died because she refused to worship the old swamis. Then another child died. He insisted that she must forsake the new religion; he tied her to a tree and beat her; he dragged her about the ground by the hair, so that bunches of her hair remained in his hand. Through it all her faith in God and His mercy has not failed. Her husband has left her and gone away with another woman. Take her into school."

This instance is one of the bright lights that illumine the scene. Does any one care to enquire about the shadows, the spurious characters that have entered in, the crass ignorance and the deep degradation? I was out on tour among the villages with my husband some years ago. In the shade of a tamarind grove he was preaching to a crowd of Madigas sitting before him. Twenty Christians from a village where nearly all had reverted to heathenism were before him. He had been in their village in the morning, had seen the swamis to which they were again making puja. The men had let their "juttus" grow. The women went about dirty and uncombed, quarrelling and using evil words to each other. Carrion had been brought into the village. There were filth and squalor beyond telling.

The Missionary described the condition in which he had found them, and then broke out into an appeal: "Oh, men! I am not ashamed to be the Guru of poor people, for Christ said He had come that the sick might be healed and the poor have the gospel preached to them. But when I sometimes see you in your villages, where you are weak Christians, then I have a pain in my mind, and I ask myself: 'Why has God chosen me to be the Guru of such *dirty* people?'" The men looked at each other, and the women involuntarily stroked down their unkempt hair.

But I could see, as I watched the faces of these lowest specimens of an Indian Pariah tribe, that, blunt as they were to any kind of teaching, they were not without responsiveness. I could see the shame in their faces. They were willing to listen, and this responsiveness proved that the spark of Divine life was there, for the spiritually dead cannot hear. But alas for the steep road out of many centuries of almost brute existence!

While the Missionary comes to one village of this kind, he comes to many where he can be proud of his people. Clean and tidy in their appearance and in their houses, they come out to meet him, the heads of households coming forward to do the honours of the occasion. A school-house in the village, and children proudly holding slates under their arms, give evidence of the status of the village. The Munsiff and Karnam come over to say a respectful salaam to the Dora, because the conduct of the Christians has taught them to honour this Dora and his religion. Crowds come to hear him preach, and Sudras are among them, sitting attentively on one side, saying, "It is a good religion. Let us listen."

There is an atmosphere of spiritual life and energy abroad in such a village. And the question comes: "Is there any power on earth, save Christianity, that could thus uplift a community within the short space of one generation?"

CONCLUSION

During many centuries the Dravidian village community of Southern India has remained practically unchanged in its organization. The simple wants of the villagers were met on the principle of mutual service. Content with their condition, there was a tendency to industrial and social stagnation, while the stimulating influence of competition was little known among them. Of late years disintegrating forces have been at work, and ancient Dravidian institutions are giving way to communal life on a new basis.

In the old days there were common holdings of land. Groups of craftsmen served the village, and in turn received their share of the harvest, or other payment in kind. The village as a whole was responsible for the revenue to be paid to the ruling Rajah. The English Government, at the present time, deals with the individual cultivator for the payment of revenue. Taxes are paid in coin; the system of mutual service, therefore, becomes unpopular, since each one learns to reckon the money value of his services. Instead of joint holdings of land, the evolution of individual property is in progress. Formerly lawlessness and petty warfare necessitated a state of cohesion in the village community. The peace and prosperity of the present time permits of internal rivalries; there are competition and the desire to excel. The joint interests of the old system are giving way to individual interests. There is disintegration on every hand.

The Madigas, too, are affected by these changes. They, too, are individually responsible to Government for the payment of taxes, and they therefore seek employment which yields payment in coin. There is a slow but steady breaking away from their former dependence upon the Sudras. Their serfdom as a tribe is slowly being transformed into individual service at stated wages. The Yettis, as the unpaid servants of the Karnam, are no longer looked upon as necessary adjuncts of the village administration. Their number is gradually being reduced, and their small holdings of land revert to Government, because it prefers to pay its servants in coin.

The lot of the Madigas has greatly improved. No petty Rajah can oppress them and force them into servitude. They are still the burden-bearers of the country; but not as in former times, when roads for traffic were few and railways unknown. They have a right to say how heavy a load they can carry. Nor is the Karnam the recipient of their pay. When English gentlemen first began to travel over the district, they asked the Karnam, when they heard the clamorous entreaties of the coolies for their pay, how much he was giving to them. Gradually the rates of payment were adjusted, much to the advantage of the cooley.

The Madiga is now a free British subject, though he has only a very dim realization of the fact. So far as the law can do this, the English Government has set the prædial slaves of India free. Practically the Madiga may be the serf of the Sudra, who has secured the right to his perpetual servitude in ways that are lawful according to ancient custom, and sanctioned by the laws of Manu. But in the sight of the English Government such contracts are divested of their strong element of slavery.

While formerly law courts did not exist for the Pariah, the equity of English law to-day, in principle at least, knows no distinction between man and man. With a true sense of what it owes to the despised class among its subjects, the Government of India has recently decided upon the name *Panchama*, "fifth caste," as a just and honourable designation for the tribes which have never found a place in the Hindu caste-system. Religious liberty has been ensured to all subjects of the Indian empire, and much is being done to place education within the reach of all—even of the most lowly.

Outward conditions have been created that make it possible for the Pariahs to become educated and prosperous, even though Sudra and Brahmin still regard them as outcasts. But who shall plant in their hearts the desire for advancement? Much lies in the power of environment; yet a motive within to impel forward makes environment more effective. The moral and social reformation of India depends to a large extent upon the action of internal forces.

From what source are these internal forces to be expected? Education cannot, single-handed, produce them. A desire for education must be created before its beneficent task can be said to have begun. Can religion form the motive power? When Christianity comes to the Pariahs of India, it comes not merely as a religion. If it is true to the teachings of its Founder, it comes to create a new environment, as well as to save the soul from death. Has Christianity in the case of the Madigas shown itself equal to this emergency?

The Madigas in several districts of the Telugu country have become Christians in sufficient numbers to make it possible to say that their communities have been Christianized, so far as that is possible, in the short period of thirty years. We cannot, as we regard the Christian Madiga communities, draw sharp lines of demarcation, and say: This has been achieved by the Mission, and that by the Government. The action of internal and external forces has been blended. The Mission has had a powerful ally in the

Government, and, in turn, the Mission has deserved the recognition of Government as one of the most beneficent forces within its borders.

In the districts where the movement among the Madigas toward Christianity was strongest, a social revolution on a small scale has taken place. The turning to Christianity meant a breaking away from ancient customs and associations. It meant a change in the relation of the Madiga to the village in general, but also a change in the Madiga hamlet itself. On the old tribal lines the Christian community is being built up. Vestiges of tribal characteristics are being assimilated by the new communal life on a Christian basis. The Madiga headman, and the heads of households to assist him, are now the "Peddalu," the elders, of the Christian village. But their simple village jurisdiction has undergone a complete transformation.

An ethical standard has been given to the Madigas by Christianity that is antagonistic to the old. Formerly they regarded as sin the neglect of the household and village gods, the theft that was detected, the social transgression so flagrant that it called for reproof from the Madiga headman. Now they understand that sin taints the motives of man, and renders him prone to choose that which is evil. Formerly, when a man went out to steal, he first bowed before the swami, requesting help, and promising a share in the spoil if carried away undetected. Now "Thou shalt not steal!" rings out with the unmistakable clearness of the Christian ethical code.

The hierarchy of self-appointed Gurus is supplanted by an organized band of Christian preachers. They do not expect devout reverence for their persons, nor do they sit down and say, "Boil rice! Cut a fowl! Bring sarai!" Perhaps the self-support of native churches would be further advanced if the preachers had more of the belligerent spirit of the ordinary Guru. Their connection with the Mission has given the preachers an air of self-respect which stoops neither to begging nor demanding. They do not mystify their followers with mantras and mystic formulæ. Their teaching is pure monotheism; and the ethical ideal which they place before the people is embodied in the God-man, Jesus Christ.

If the Madigas could become landholders and independent cultivators, they would soon be able to educate their children and support their preachers. The last resource left to the Sudras, as they try to keep their former serfs in their servile condition, is the attempt to frustrate any move on their part to own land and cultivate it. Even though a Madiga may come into possession of land, the Sudras have means of putting obstacles in his way, so that only with great difficulty can he raise his crops.

The Mission, aided liberally by Government, has provided general education for the Madigas. At Ongole there is even opportunity for the Madiga lad to obtain a college education. But the important moral factor of self-help is lacking. Many families are so poor that they regard it as a sacrifice, however gladly offered, when they send their sons and daughters to school, instead of keeping them at home to help earn cooley for the family. Not until they are able to carry the financial burdens of the new communal life, that has been grafted upon the old, will they gain the full benefit of Christian civilization.

Industrial education could do much toward further emancipating the Madiga. The only industry now known to him is leather work, done with crude tools, according to ancient usage. This need also the Mission is beginning to meet.

Has Christianity been equal to the task of furnishing the motive for the social as well as religious regeneration of the Madigas? Emphatically it has. The Madigas say: "Our ancestress, Arunzodi, cursed us, saying, '*Though you work and toil, it shall not raise your condition. Unclothed and untaught you shall be, ignorant and despised, the slaves of all.*' During many centuries the curse rested heavily upon us. Christianity has removed it. It is no more."

REFERENCES

A Comparative Grammar of the Dravidian or South Indian Family of Languages. Rev. R. Caldwell, D.D., LL.D. London, 1875. Second Edition.

The Indian Village Community. B. H. Baden-Powell, M.A., C.I.E. 1896.

On the Original Inhabitants of Bharatavarsa, or India. Gustav Oppert, Ph.D. 1893.

Tree and Serpent Worship. J. Fergusson, D.C.L., M.R.A.S. 1873.

Religious Thought and Life in India. Sir Monier Williams. 1885.

Genealogie der Malabarischen Götter. B. Ziegenbalg. 1867. See p. 157, Legend of Ellama; p. 42, Enumeration of Saktis.

The Shaktas. H. H. Wilson, LL.D. *Calcutta Review*, No. 47. 1855.

Hindu Manners, Customs, and Ceremonies. Abbé J. A. Dubois. 1897.

Memorandum on the Progress of the Madras Presidency during the last Forty Years of British Administration. S. Srinivasa Raghavaiyangar, B.A., C.I.E. 1893.

New India; or, India in Transition. H. J. S. Cotton, Bengal Civil Service. 1885.

A Manual of the Administration of the Madras Presidency. 1886.

A Manual of Coorg. Rev. G. Richter. 1870.

The Ramayana of Valmiki. Translated by Manmatha Nath Dutt, M.A. Calcutta, 1892. See Books III. and IV.

The Mahabharata, Anusana-parvan. Verses 1872 ff.

The Dynasties of the Kanarese Districts of the Bombay Presidency, by J. F. Fleet. 1882. See p. 10. A later edition of the same work, to be found in the *Official Gazetteer of the Bombay Presidency*, vol. i. part ii. 1896. See p. 293. A picture of the Canarese inscription, deciphered by Mr. Fleet, is found in *The Indian Antiquary*, vol. viii. p. 241. 1879.

The Kadambari of Bana. Translated from the Sanscrit by C. M. Ridding. 1896. See pp. 30, 31.

The Katha Sarit Sagara; or, Ocean of the Streams of Story. By Sri Somadeva Bhatta. Translated from the Sanscrit by C. H. Tawney, M.A. 1880. Two volumes. See Matanga in the Index.

The Mackenzie Collection, Calcutta, 1828. By H. H. Wilson. See vol. ii. p. 41. In the Nalakanara books of local history the "female warrior Matangi" occurs.

Customs of the Comti Caste. Major J. S. F. Mackenzie. 1878. *The Indian Antiquary*, vol viii. p. 36.

On the Study of the South Indian Vernaculars. Rev. G. U. Pope, D.D. *Journal Royal Asiatic Society*. XVII., New Series, p. 163. 1885. See the story of the poet, Tiruvalluvar.

An Account of the Religious Opinions and Observances ot the Khonds of Gumsoor and Boad. Captain S. E. Macpherson. *Journal Royal Asiatic Society*, vol. vii. 1843.

Remarks on the Origin and History of the Parawas. Simon Casie Chetty. *Journal Royal Asiatic Society*, vol. iv. 1837.

The Geography of Rama's Exile. F. E. Pargiter, B.A. *Journal Royal Asiatic Society*. 1894.

The Rig Veda, Mandala x. 85. See the Bridal Hymn.

Samkhya und Yoga. R. Garbe. Encyclopædia of Indo-Aryan Research. 1896.

The Religions of India. A. Barth. 1882. See p. 202 on Mother-worship.

From Darkness to Light. The Story of a Telugu. Rev J. E. Clough, D.D. Boston. 1882. Third edition.

The History of the Telugu Mission of the American Baptist Missionary Union. Rev. D. Downie, D.D. Philadelphia. 1893. This book gives the history of the Mission in general, of which Ongole is a part. During a period of thirty years the pioneers of the Telugu Mission believed that, "God has a great people among the Telugus," while but few cared for their message. Rev. Lyman Jewett, D.D., visited Ongole repeatedly, when the Mission had but its one station, at Nellore. In 1865, after pleading with the Society at home not to abandon the field, though barren and hard, he returned to India with Rev. J. E. Clough, D.D., and his wife, the missionaries for Ongole. During the first ten years at Ongole, a town situated 180 miles north of Madras, near the coast, the foundations were laid, there was a steady increase, and when the famine of 1876–8 began, the Ongole Church counted 3,269 members. In July, 1878, within three days, 3,536 were baptized, and during that year 9,606 were added to the Church at Ongole. In 1883, the Church membership had increased to 21,000, and the nominal adherents counted from four to five times that number. The first division of the large field was therefore imperative. The four Taluks—small counties—lying farthest away from Ongole were made separate stations. Ten years later the work at Ongole had again assumed unwieldy proportions, when a second similar division took place. The movement spread, and to-day the Mission counts twenty-six stations, with a membership of 53,748. Nearly all of these have come from the Madigas living in the Nellore, Kurnool, and Kistnah districts of the Telugu country. The Census of 1891 gives the total number of Christians in the American Baptist Telugu Mission as 84,158, by counting many of the adherents.

THE NUMERICAL STATUS OF THE MADIGAS.

The entire population of India, 287,223,431.

The Leather Workers of India.

Northern India	Chamars	11,258,105
	Mochis	961,133
Southern India	Madigas	927,339
	Chakilyans	445,366
Central India	Bambhi	220,596
		13,812,539
Other Pariahs in India		7,157,740
The entire Pariah population of India		20,970,279
The Telugu population of Southern India		17,003,358

The Madigas are the leather workers of the Telugu country, and as a large proportion of the Chakilyans, the leather workers of the Tamil country, speak Telugu, they appear to be immigrants from the Telugu districts.

(From the Census of 1891.)

INDEX

Aborigines and Aryans, 16, 25.
— chieftainship of, 29.
— cults of, 16, 89, 105.
— and Siva, 84, 117.
— and Vishnu, 116.
— and human sacrifice, 75, 101.
— and English law, 217, 305.
Adimata, 63.
Adijambuvu, 13–20, 30, 41.
Adisakti, 14, 16.
Adisesha, 72, 74.
Adivaramu, 63.
Agastya, 55.
Aihole, temple at, 23.
Ankalamah, 77, 122, 195, 214.
Arminian doctrine, 107.
Arundhati, 55.
Arunzodi, 54–57, 310.
Aryan race, 9.
— cults, 82, 117.
— conquests, 9, 13.
— hermits, 10, 16, 21, 82.
— customs, 11, 31, 174, 190.
Asceticism, 58, 81.
Atri, 55.

Baal, groves of, 74.
Bainurdu, the, 64, 69.
Banabhatta, 25, 102.
Baputla Taluk, 159.
Bhang, 163.
Bhagavata Purana, 233.
Bhagvatam, 223, 227.
Blumenbach, 8.
Brahma and Adijambuvu, 14.
— and Yogi doctrine, 162.
Brahminical exaggerations, 12, 29, 59.
— hierarchy, 11, 80, 88.
— settlers, 12, 34.
Brahmins, the, intrigue of, 34.
— feast for, 29.
— legend about, 49, 52–55, 85.
— and Madigas, 39, 216, 253.
— and Chandalas, 80.
— and Matangi cult, 64, 76.

Brahmins and aboriginal cults, 82, 89.
Buddhist doctrines, 75, 101.
Buffalo, legend of a, 49.
Bundelkhand, 18.

Cabaras, the, 25.
Caldwell, 9.
Calvinistic doctrine, 107.
Canarese country, 17.
— inscription, 23.
— language, 10.
Carrion-eating, 41, 151, 185, 247, 291.
Caste, development of, 11, 32.
— loss of, 251.
— in Nasriah sect, 164.
— and reformers, 163, 222.
— and Madigas, 35, 197, 222, 253.
Caucasian race, 9.
Chalukya dynasty, 23.
Chandala element, 78.
— maiden, 28.
— origin, 78, 88.
Chermanishta sect, 103–109, 220, 227.
Coorg, 59–61.

Dandaka, the forest, 18, 26, 80.
Dasiri, Madiga, 55, 190.
Dasyus, 10.
Delhi, 88.
Dewan, 36, 38.
Dora—gentleman, 113, 138, 148, 187, 211, 236, 252.
Dorasani—lady, 114, 148, 189, 282.
Dravidian racial affinity, 8, 61.
— customs, 11.
— literature, 10, 21.
— dynasties, 18, 23, 33.
— tribes, 8, 32, 44, 59, 94.
— village community, 31 302.
Drums, Madiga, 209, 215
Dubois, Abbé, 101.
Durga, 102.
Durgapisacha, King, 27.
Dyaus, 73.

Ellama, possessed by, 63.
— and the great Saktis, 78.
— legend of, 84–86.
— worshippers of, 181, 297.

Family cohesion, 6.
Famine, 271–284.
Fleet, J. F., 24.

Gandharvas, the, 85.
Gheras, the, 18.
Godavery district, 120, 135.
Goomsur, 91.

Government, English, and human sacrifice, 75, 101.
— and famine relief, 274, 283.
— and taxes, 303.
— and Rajah of Goomsur, 91.
— and Madigas, 35, 126, 217, 254, 306.
Gundlacumma river, 66.
Gurus—religious teachers, customs of, 131, 144, 168.
— incident of, 133, 169.
— reverence for, 144, 167, 308.
— teaching of, 104, 115, 119, 157.
— worthlessness of, 131, 135.

Haeckel, 8.
Hanuman, 20.
Headman, Sudra, 33.
— Madiga, 44, 64, 143, 172.
Holdings of land, 32, 304.
Hymns of the Nasriah sect, 170, 175, 184.
— Christian, 184, 289.
— bridal, in Rig Veda, 55.

Idols, 164, 168, 176, 226, 238, 241.
Immortality, 202–206.
Incompatibility, social, 16.
Indra, 10, 80.
Inscriptions, 22.

Jamadagni, 72, 86.
Jambavan, 17–20.
Jambavanta, 17.
Jambu, 17.
Juttu—lock of hair—significance of, 145, 151, 292, 299.
— incident of cutting, 145, 196, 215.

Kali, 102.
Kamadhenu, 12–15.
Kanigiri Taluk, 120.
Karnam, the office of, 33.
— persecution by, 210.
— and Yetti, 37, 205, 303.
— and Madigas, 252, 304.
Katachchuris, the, 23.
Kausika, 55.
Kaveri river, 84.
Khonds, the, 94.
Kolarian race, 8.
Komati Chetty, dishonesty of, 277.
— marriage customs of, 47.
— wealth of, 46.
— as money-lenders, 46, 133.
Krishna, the god, 218, 225.
Krishna river, 18, 68.
Kshatriyas, 34.
Kumara Rama, 87.

Kurral, the, 57, 59.

Lanka, the island, 19.
Legends, trustworthiness of, 24.
— of Adijambuvu, 13–20.
— of Arunzodi, 54–57.
— of Ellama, 84–86.
— of the Komatis, 49.
— of the Matangi, 71.
— of Vasugi, 57.
— of woman in Coorg, 60.
— of Veerabramham, 118.
Lemuria, 9.
Logan, 9.

Mackenzie, Major, 48.
Madiga, derivation of name, 23.
— clannish spirit of, 145, 179.
— headman, 44, 143, 172.
— idea of immortality, 202.
— poverty of, 42.
Madras, 91, 274.
Madras Presidency, 50, 94.
Madura, 57.
Mahabharata, 79.
Mahalakshmi, 91–94, 194.
Malas, relation to Madigas, 185, 222.
— priests among, 219, 246.
Malabar, 59–61, 78, 86.
Malayalim language, 10.
Mangalisa, 22.
Mansion House Fund, 284.
Mantras—prayers, 145, 170, 226, 239.
Manu, laws of, 305.
Marriage customs, 40, 47, 56 189.
Matanga, *masc.*, interpretation of, 23, 79, 88.
— the king, 27.
— the sage, 79.
— the ascetic, 80.
— the leader, 25.
Matangi, *fem.*, interpretation of, 23, 63, 79, 88.
— -Makkalu, 24.
— and Komatis, 48.
— displeasure of, 182.
— description of cult, 62–76.
— in legends, 79–89.
— the female warrior, 87.
Matriarchate, 73.
Matris—mothers, 99, 178, 209.
Migrankadatta, 27.
Miraculous power of Nasriah, 163.
— of Arunzodi, 54.
— of Vasugi, 58.
— of woman in Coorg, 60.
Mohammed the Third, 87.
Mohammedan, 87, 159, 211.
Mongolian race, 9.
Munsiff, the, office of, 32.

Munsiff, persecution by, 248–263.
— mother of a, 177.
Mysore district, 48.

Naga, 180.
Nagarpamah, 180.
Narsaravapetta, 160.
Nasriah the reformer, 158–161.
— sect, 162–165.
— and Christianity, 204.
— discussion on, 194.

Ornaments of women, 189, 191.
— of men, 130.
Oudh, the house of, 18.

Pallavas, the, 18.
Pampa, the lake, 81.
Panchama, 305.
Parameswara, 220.
Parasu-Rama, 84.
Parawas, the, 83.
Pariah, 16, 46, 55, 61, 78, 85, 305.
Parvati, 71, 73, 83, 89, 106, 214.
Penoocondah, 50.
Perantalu, description of, 99, 100.
— incident of, 179.
Podili Taluk, 38.
Poleramah, 122, 194, 250, 267.
Polygamy, 149.
Polytheism, 5.
Possession, dance of, 65–69, 93, 251.
Pothuluri Veerabramham, 117, 135, 222.
Prithivi, 73.
Puja—worship, sacrifice, 97, 142, 181, 225, 239, 281.
Puranas, the, 83, 102, 233.

Rakshasas, the, 19.
Rajah and King Matanga 28.
— visits of, 36.
— grants from, 36, 205.
— taxes levied by, 29, 39.
— of Goomsur, 91–93.
— of Venkatagiri, 205.
Rajayogi sect, teaching of, 115, 127.
— disciples of, 117, 135, 146, 220.
Rama, prayer to, 118.
— and Jambavan, 18.
— and Savari, 80–82.
Ramanujacarya, 107, 219.
Ramanuja sect, explanation of, 106–109.
— and Madigas, 116.
— priests of, 116, 219.
Ramaswami, 141, 153.

Ramayana, the, 17, 80, 82, 233.
Ravana, 19.
Reddis, the, 65.
Re-incarnation, 83, 118.
Reformers, 117, 163.
Rig Veda, 10, 55, 73.
Rishis, 10.

Sacrifice, 66, 75, 92, 101.
Saivism, 84, 89.
Saktis, the ten great, 77, 78, 102, 214.
Saktism in Nasriah sect, 164.
— and Matangi cult, 73.
— and Perantalu, 100.
— and Chermanishta sect, 105.
Sanscrit authors, 25, 26.
— academy, 57.
— dictionaries, 56.
— epics, 22, 79, 80.
— dialects, 11.
— learning, 16, 21, 224.
Sanyasi, 162, 168.
Sarai—arrack, 134, 144, 163, 185, 291.
Scythian, 9, 73, 95.
Sect, Nasriah, 158–166, 194.
— Chermanishta, 103–109, 220, 227.
— Ramanuja, 106, 116, 219.
— Rajayogi, 117, 146, 220.
Serfdom, 39.
Serpent worship, antiquity of, 73, 180.
— — and Matangi cult, 73.
— — and human sacrifice 75.
Shastra, 26, 127.
Sita, 18–20.
Siva, curse of, 29.
— worshipper of, 64, 118, 214, 220.
— consort of, 71, 73, 83, 106.
— and Dravidians, 14, 83, 89.
Slavery, 35.
Somadeva Bhatta, 26.
Sudra servant, 34, 37.
— landholder, 39, 208.
— opinion, 7, 122, 153.
— caste, 34, 65.
— and Ellama, 64.
— and Madigas, 40, 207, 248, 303.
Sugriva, 19.
Swami—god, 97, 171, 215, 239.

Talibottu, 189.
Taluk—a small county, 65, 120, 159.
Tamil, 10, 57.
Tamurdu—younger brother, 213.
Taxes, 29, 39, 303.
Telugu, 10, 87.
Teutons, the, 74.

Theism, 5.
Tiruvalluvar, 57.
Tiprantakamu, 158, 165, 193.
Totems, 18.
Trade, 133, 136, 184.
Triamballa, King, 83.
Tribe, institutions of, 32, 307.
— distinctness of, 6, 44.
— records of, 22.
— wars of, 31.
— head of, 17, 21, 30.

Ursa Major, 56.

Valavisu Purana, 83.
Valluvas, the, 16.
Vaishnavism, 84, 89.
Vaishnavite reformers, 107, 219.
Vaisya traders, 34, 50.
Vasishta, 55.
Vasugi, 57–59.
Vellamanu, 13–16.
Venkatagiri, Rajah of, 205.
Venkateswarurdu, 238.
Vijayanagar, 50.
Village community, 31, 210, 302.
Vishnu, consort of, 108.
— worshipper of, 64, 220.
— incarnations of, 116.
Vishnu, idols of, 116, 164.
— and positive evil, 95.

Widowhood enforced, 174.
— and ornaments, 190.
— of caste women, 99.
Woman and gods, 99.
— and forces of nature, 61, 100.
— the Aryan, 18, 59.
Worship of nature, 73, 105.
— of the serpent, 67, 73.
— of trees, 74.
— of demons, 95, 203.
— of matris, 99.
— of Perantalu, 99, 179.
— of Nagarpamah, 181.
— of Sakti, 73, 180.

Yetti, the, and the Rajah, 36.
— — and the Karnam, 37, 208, 249, 303.
— — as news-bearers, 147, 171, 173, 263.
— — as bearers of letters, 37, 205.
Yogi, the, doctrine, 162, 164.
— teachers, 5, 117.
— practice, 120.

Ziegenbalg, B., 78, 86.